Phoenix Rising

By Dr. Rose Bruce

Copyright © 2021 Dr. Rose Bruce

All rights reserved. No part of this publication may be reproduced, distributed, or transmitted in any form or by any means, including photocopying, recording, or other electronic or mechanical methods, without the prior written permission of the publisher, except in the case of brief quotations embodied in critical reviews and certain other noncommercial uses permitted by copyright law. For permission requests, write to the publisher, addressed "Attention: Book Rights and Permission," at the address below.

Published in the United States of America

ISBN 978-1-953904-57-7 (SC)

Dr. Rose Bruce
Rose Bruce 7697
Isabel Drive Cotati, CA 94931
www.RoseSobriety.com

Ordering Information and Rights Permission:
Quantity sales. Special discounts might be available on quantity purchases by corporations, associations, and others. For details, contact the publisher at the address above.

For Book Rights Adaptation and other Rights Permission. Call us at toll free 1-888-945-8513 or send us email at admin@stellarliteray.com.

*"The I AM works through us
to will and to do that which ought to be done by us."
Emma Curtis Hopkins*

Oh Thou, Who givest sustenance to the universe, From Whom all things proceed,
To Whom all things return,
Unveil to us the face of the True Spiritual Son/Sun, Hidden by a disk of golden light,
That we may know the Truth, And do our whole duty,
As we journey to Thy Sacred Feet.
Prelude to A Prince Song Circle of Fire

Contents

Dedication IX
Forward To Part One X
Foreword To Part Two XI

PART ONE 13
   My Life 14
   Another Unexpected Twist 17
   Gary 20
   Checklist of Health Issues and Illnesses (CHII) 27
   Meditation 31
   Leslie 33
   Learning About Alcoholism 37
   The Third Step Prayer 39
   Dreams and Guidance 40
   Eric 41
   A New Car 44
   A New Book to Read 45
   God's Will 46
   The Sacred Heart 48
   Depression 50
   Higher Power 53
   Spiritual School 54

2017 in Review *55*

Dreams, Being Broken, and Blackouts *57*

Message From Leslie *59*

Death *60*

A Progressive Disease *62*

Fear *63*

The Rhythm of My Week *64*

Bless Her and Change Me *66*

Hope and Joy *68*

Suicidal Thoughts *69*

You Don't Do It Alone *71*

Being Secretary *72*

H & I *73*

It's My Disease Talking *74*

Similarities Not Differences *76*

My Sponsor *79*

Friends *81*

Alzheimer's *82*

Uncertainty *85*

My Private Safe Place *88*

My Heart *90*

Surrender *92*

Gratitude *94*

Living in the Presence *96*

Doubt *97*

Being of Service *99*

Intellectual Influences on the Twelve Steps *101*

PART TWO 106

The Center for Spiritual Living *107*

Old Thought vs. New Thought *109*

Spirit, Mind, Body *112*

Healing *113*

Spiritual Mind Treatment *115*

Projections *117*

Seed Thought *119*

Women's Retreat *121*

Guided Meditation in the Redwood Glen *123*

A Spirit Walk *124*

Four Swans Flying *125*

A Near Fatal Car Crash *126*

Response Paper on Thomas Troward *128*

Our Bloated Nothingness *130*

Becky *132*

Still Fires *135*

Spiritual Guidance and Discernment *137*

Scientific Christian: Mental Practice By Emma Curtis Hopkins [20] *139*

Spiritual Roots of Science of Mind *141*

Thanksgiving *143*

A Dinner Party *144*

A Christmas Tree *146*

A Tree Fell *148*
A Dream *150*
The Dinner Party *152*
Christmas *154*
My Support System *156*
The New Year *158*
Divine Love *160*
Spiritual Mind Treatment To Release Worry *162*
Spiritual Mind Treatment for Forgiveness *164*
Moss and Ferns *166*
Thursdays *168*
Spiritual Mind Treatment To Be True To Oneself *170*
Spiritual Mind Treatment For Surgery *172*
Spiritual Mind Treatment for Rose *174*
What is Spiritual Mind Treatment? *176*
My Prayer Partner *179*
Show Me The Way *180*

The Ending 181
Appendix A The Twelve Steps of Recovery
.... 182
Appendix B References 184

Dedication

This book is dedicated to all women who may have known marriage, divorce, domestic violence, perfectionism, thirst for spiritual understanding, the love of a man, the love of a woman, retirement, death of a spouse, alcoholism, training in Martial Arts, Higher Education, worldwide travel and a generally successful life and career. In other words, women who have lived a nontraditional life in America. Women who have challenged traditional boundaries and role expectations in society. Women who have known defeat and have learned from it. Women who have survived life's hardships and challenges and made it to the other side with hope and renewal. My story is not unique, but it is mine. Like a Phoenix rising from the ashes, I have learned to transcend many challenges in my life.

This book is also dedicated to my sponsor and all those who selflessly gave of their time, knowledge and love to help me in my journey of Recovery from alcoholism. It is dedicated to all those who still suffer. I would also like to thank all of my teachers at The Center for Spiritual Living in Santa Rosa, California who gave tirelessly to me and the other students in the classes I took there: Reverend Edward Viljoen, Reverend Joyce Duffala, Elias Owens, and Reverend Ruth Barnhart. My understanding of Science of Mind grew gradually under the insight and nurturance of these wonderful people. I feel truly blessed.

This book is also dedicated to all those who are interested in Science of Mind and a spiritual life. It is a rich topic with many wonderful authors to read. This book mentions a few of them. Blessings to you on your road to spiritual understanding and insight.

Forward to Part One

It is a pleasure to write this foreword for Rose Bruce. I have known Rose for over ten years (the last two as her therapist). I've watched her ups and downs as she has dealt with great loss, and significant emotional challenge. Rose is a highly intelligent, successful career woman and educator with numerous talents, high energy and a keen spiritual curiosity. She's also an alcoholic.

Once Rose started the 12 Step Program of Recovery she delved deeply into her search for understanding of the disease, and her own descent into it. She has made a sincere search for self-awareness, humility and spiritual connection. This has meant a leap in her well-being, improvement in all her relationships and the foundation of her equanimity. I have been witness to Rose's changes in the last year and it is rare that I see someone dedicate themselves so earnestly and completely to their Recovery as she.

This book started as a journal for her own healing, for her Recovery, and as a record of her experiences. Her decision to turn her own journal/journey into a book for the public comes from her desire to be of service. I think you will find it as engaging and informative as I have.

If you or anyone you know struggles with the disease of alcoholism this book will educate and inspire through the narrative journey of this singular woman.

Frances Fuchs, PHD
April, 2018

Foreword To Part Two

A life well-lived balances both action and reflection. Action is obviously necessary to get things done. Reflection allows us to thoughtfully consider what we are about to do, and to learn from and improve upon what we have just done. Reflection ensures that our actions will be for the highest ethical good for as many people as possible, including ourselves.

You no doubt can think of ready examples of people you know – either personally or by public repute – who seem to jump into action without much reflection. Perhaps, like me, you may have made this mistake yourself at some time. I think we can agree that the results of too much action and not enough reflection are not optimal, and can even be disastrous.

What follows this foreword are the writings of a woman who has become quite masterful in the art of reflection, Dr. Rose Bruce. In this book, she reflects on previous life experiences, daily activities, and her new-found study of the work of 20th Century religious philosopher, Ernest Holmes, relating them all to her own spiritual philosophy of life.

I first met Rose Bruce in January 2019, when I was teaching a class at the Center for Spiritual Living, Santa Rosa entitled "Basic Principles of Science of Mind." This class is an introduction to Holmes's spiritual philosophy, and draws spiritual explorers from a diverse range of background and experience.

It quickly became obvious that Rose was a woman of rich experience and study, as evidenced by her thought-provoking questions, wisdom-filled statements, and committed drive to explore the material. It came as no surprise, then, when I found out Rose held two doctorates, and was a published author.

Touching again on the value of reflection, not only does it inform our actions,.reflection is also a key element when we are learning a new body of knowledge. Reflection moves us from "I understand this intellectually" to "I personally find meaning in this for my own life." I am grateful that Rose continues to find personal meaning in her expanding understanding of Science of Mind, and has so generously offered us the wisdom gleaned from her reflections on this philosophy in the context of her very rich and thoughtful life.

Joyce Duffala, Ed.D
Assistant Minister,
Center for Spiritual Living, Santa Rosa, April, 2020

PART ONE

My Life

My life has been a series of personal challenges and opportunities, disappointments and recoveries, the depths of despair and the joys of love and accomplishments. At each juncture, I felt like my life was over, and indeed that chapter of it was. What I had difficulty seeing at that time was that with the destruction of one life structure, another one was being born. The rebirth was oftentimes a hard and arduous labor, but I did survive and even thrive in the next phase. And in the end, like a phoenix rising, I would find the awe and wonder in the world again. Usually that transition took several years to accomplish. This book recounts my story.

I was brought up in a Swedish Lutheran family from Kansas. We had wonderful traditional Swedish holidays, church every week, emphases on the importance of education, love and support. It was a comfortable and stable home life. I had two older sisters. From ages six to sixteen we lived on a lake and I was able to swim, paddle board, ski, and enjoy the wonderful outdoors. I was a tomboy and very good at school.

All I knew about alcohol was that we drank it at dinner at Easter and Christmas (when I was an adult). I could have one drink of wine or maybe two. But that was it.

I was raised to be a wife and a mother. I married at 19 as had my mother and my two sisters before me. However, for me, that ended when my husband of four years walked out of the marriage suddenly. I came home from work one summer day and he was not there. There was no note and I couldn't understand where he was. I looked in the closet and saw that his clothes were gone. I called the bank and was told that he had withdrawn half of our checking and savings account. I was devastated, shocked and felt ill. I was numb for several months and tried desperately to figure out what to do.

My parents told me that the divorce was my fault. That did not feel accurate to me. My dad took me to talk to their minister and I felt totally misunderstood and judged. I realized I was on my own in figuring out who I was now that the traditional path of my life had so drastically changes. I decided to take a trip with a new male friend, who had lived in Spain for two years and was fluent in Spanish, through Mexico, Central and South America. We hopped into my dark green 1968 VW Bug with license plate SDS069 and left to see the world. I had always wanted to travel, probably spurred on by my Dad's stories of being a pilot in WW II in Italy. I had taken a trip to Europe and then Turkey with my husband. It was seven months before we came back from down South to home to California. During that time, I had time to reflect, to read about and start doing hatha yoga and to realize that everything I had been taught was relative to the culture I had been raised up in. I learned some Spanish and talked with women as we travelled from town to town. I would ask them about their lives, hopes and dreams. They usually did not have any hopes and dreams and rather they felt certain that they would spend the rest of their lives in, the hot dusty town they were born in. They were probably right. I realized I had many options being born White, a woman, and in America. I felt a huge sense of responsibility to do something with my life and I decided to return to college.

I shopped around for colleges in Northern California. I was into Tarot Cards at that time and whenever I asked about one college in particular, the Sun card would come up which is a Major Arcana card that represents "attaining the highest spiritual level." I didn't know what that meant exactly but felt it implied that good things were ahead. So, I moved to a small town in the valley of California to attend a State University. Because of the sudden dissolution of my marriage, I was interested in Psychology to understand what had happened in my life. I got my Bachelor's and Master's degrees (in

Psychology and Counseling respectively). I lived alone in a small house my folks had bought for me to stay in while going to school and loved it. I could do anything I wanted to day or night. I was finally getting to know who I was in this new phase of life and feel comfortable being "me."

Another Unexpected Twist

While getting my BA and MA, I started studying the Martial Art of Kodenkan Ju Jitsu. Three evenings a week and Saturday mornings I would be at the Dojo for two-hour classes. It was extremely challenging physically and mentally. However, I liked the ability to throw men on the ground and to kick the punching bag. I was also dating my Ju Jitsu instructor at the time, and he did not coddle me. I remember returning from one class early on when I was learning how to fall (like in Aikido). I was bruised from head to toe. I wanted to stay home from class the next night and he said "you go to class no matter what." I learned how to be self-disciplined and go to class no matter what my emotional or physical state – to push myself.

In Ju Jitsu, we work in pairs. We learn to throw each other, fall on the mat, put on holds and release. As time went on, I got better. When a new, macho man would come into the Dojo, he was paired with me. If he threw me down hard into the mat, I would not say a thing. I would proceed to throw him hard into the mat. That way he learned, without me saying anything, how to be gentle. I did my Master's Thesis on the personality characteristics of White Belters compared to Black Belters in the Ju Jitsu Federation in the United States (administering the *Edwards Personal Preference Schedule* - EPPS). The difference was that as women progressed through the ranks, they learned to be self-reliant and independent. You were all alone on the mat, no one could do it but you. Women Black Belters scored as high as Women Olympic Competitors. Conversely, men learned to be sensitive to their partner and cooperative.

Ju Jitsu was a healthy way to get out my anger at the male prejudice I was experiencing in society. I also had a lot of anger at my first husband. After four years I was promoted to Shodan, 1st Degree Black Belt. I studied another two years after that. I gained self- confidence. I also learned Japanese massage, called the Okasaki Long Life Massage after the Founder of the System, and used that to support myself during the next phase of my life. Professor Okasaki studies in Japan then moved to Hawaii where he taught Bud Estes, who bought the knowledge to the U.S. In Ju Jitsu the philosophy was that whatever could be broken could be healed. We learned many traditional methods to heal injuries. Professor Estes, the Head of the System, or 10th Dan, taught massage techniques to the public. He also privately was called upon by members of the community to heal them, which he did for free. He treated headaches, backaches and menstrual cramps. I had the opportunity to spend one summer going with him on his many home visits after work. That was the summer before his death. We were quite close.

After graduating and working for about a year and a half at the college I had attended, I decided it was time to get more education to promote my professional career. At that time, I was interested in becoming a counselor so I decided to enroll in a private doctoral program in Clinical Psychology in Berkeley, California, commuting between the town I lived in and there. I was supporting myself by doing message by appointment in the dojo which I helped to run. This was a type of full body message designed to promote general health that I had learned when I was studying Ju Jitsu. I had very little money but I felt I was on the right track.

Then suddenly my life fell apart again. I had a series of three dreams a week in a row the nights before I would return home from Berkeley. The first one was innocuous enough just a Black Belter friend talking to me. But it happened verbatim as I had dreamed. I didn't know what that meant, but I trusted the next two dreams when they occurred. The last one was of my then husband of a year and a half, my Ju Jitsu instructor, being with another woman. That weekend I found him with that woman and realized that that marriage was over. I again was shocked and devastated and did not know what to do.

Gary

I met Gary when I was working at Tower Books and Records while going to school for my Bachelors and Master's degree. I worked the noon to midnight shift a few days a week in the books and paraphernalia part of the store. One night a fellow employee who worked during the day came in. I immediately felt an attraction to him. Gary was tall, 6' 8, and handsome. He was half Cherokee on his Mother's side. Because we worked different shifts, I seldom saw him. I knew he had a girlfriend and I had a boyfriend at the time. Occasionally he would stop by alone and ask if I wanted to take a break with him. I would say "yes" and we would drive through Bidwell Park in his VW van. He would smoke a joint and we would talk. I never enjoyed smoking pot so would decline his offer for some. He had a calm manner and I liked him very much.

One night his girlfriend was out of town and he asked me if I would like to go to a friend's house for the evening who was out of town. I went. We took a long hot bath together and made love in a slow sensuous manner. It was heavenly. I had to leave early that morning and the song by Tom Waits seemed to describe the experience exactly:

Oh the night went so quickly and I went lickety splickity

Out to my old '65.

As I pulled away slowly, feeling so holy, God knows I was feeling alive. And now the sun's coming up I'm riding with Lady Luck, freeways cars and trucks.

Stars beginning to fade, and I lead the parade, just a wishing I'd

Stayed a little longer. Lord knows don't you know that the feeling's getting stronger.

It was so wonderful and I longed to spend more nights like that one.

It was some time before that was to happen again and under totally different circumstances. I had decided to enroll in a Clinical Doctoral program in Berkeley and live in the small college town where I had gotten my Bachelor's and Master's degree. My husband at that time left me suddenly and I recall one rainy winter evening when my car windshield washers did not work, and I felt totally alone and afraid. I pulled into where I thought he lived and knocked on the door. He answered, took one look at me, and pulled me into the comfort of his warm embrace. I felt safe, protected and happy. I wanted to stay there forever. And thus, our romance was rekindled and we began to see each other on a regular basis.

To make a long story short, we continued to date throughout that Spring. I would share what I was learning in the Clinical Program and he would listen attentively while we were listening to wonderful music like the Grateful Dead and the Moody Blues. It was the 1970s in California. I thought that he was supportive of my career plans and understood the emotions I was trying to explain during our long conversations. He asked me to marry him and I said "yes." When it came time for me to register for the next year in the Clinical Program, he got furious with me and said that, of course, I would not be going on in the program because we were getting married. I felt confused but weak and said that I would stop the program. That began the first real problem drinking for me and I ended up in Recovery for a short time. But after a few months I was tempted to have a glass of wine at dinner with his parents and I slowly grew away from Recovery.

When we were first getting together and making love one night, I kept flashing on a scene where he and I were together making love. We were both American Indians. We had two children. I believe we have been together in another lifetime and that is why the pull was so strong when I met him. Also, when I went to see a healer after his death (see Chapter on Death), she commented after the session that she had never felt such strong love between two people.

We moved to a county in Northern California and I got a job at a Drug

Abuse Agency scheduling Intakes. One day a counselor in the program, who was looking for work at the university in that town, said to me there was an opening for a psychometrist (a person who understands psychological measurement theory and statistical methods) and hadn't I done that before? Yes, I had and the job application had to be turned in the next day. I applied and got the job. I now see that my Higher Power was intervening in my life to set my life on a new path. I started working there and remained there for 30 years. I gradually got stronger in myself partly because that was required of me in my professional position.

I was told that I needed to get a doctoral degree to advance in my profession. So, I shopped around and found the perfect program for me at the University of California at Berkeley. It was in the School of Education with an emphasis on quantitative methods in Educational Psychology. It was possible for me to commute to Berkeley and return to work in the same day. I was given one day a week of release time to attend classes and decided I wanted to attend the doctoral program. I had to spend about eighty hours a week commuting, working, and doing homework. Saturday was our day together. My husband had not changed his mind about me getting an advanced degree and did not support this plan. I took him to talk with my supervisor at the time who explained why I needed the degree. That still did not convince him. However, I had grown stronger in myself and was determined that I would go. At lunch one day I told him that I was going to enroll in the doctoral program. He said "if you are going to go to school then I want you to buy me a sports car." I said o.k. and we went and bought a red Pontiac Fiero. He was free to cruise around and I was free to go back to school. Fortunately, I had just received a raise at work which covered these two new monthly costs.

After six years I got my Doctorate in Education, EdD, from the University of California at Berkeley. When I finished my doctoral studies, I was promoted to the Director of the Testing Office at the University where I worked. I continued to work there until my retirement 30 years later holding several positions of increasing responsibility along the way. When I retired, I was the Associate Vice President of Institutional Research.

Gary and I loved to travel. We would take our Federal Income Tax Return of about $3,000 each year and go on a trip. We went to Hawaii, Mexico, Europe, St. Thomas, and Bonnaire. Our last trip together was one he won to Tavarua, a Surfing Resort in Fiji. It was magical.

As the years went by, I slowly began to experience a part of Gary's personality that I had not seen in the beginning. He became progressively possessive of me and my time and attention. He would insist that I come home from work immediately and would question me if I were even fifteen minutes late insisting that I must be having an affair. Of course, nothing could have been farther from the truth. I now think that he was starting to have affairs on me and that is why he reacted this way. He became more and more controlling feeling threatened if I even looked at another man and smiled in a friendly manner. I did not understand what was happening.

As you might expect, the abuse eventually became physical and at one point ended up with him strangling me on the living room couch after I had announced to him that I was not going to take this behavior any more. After each episode I would feel ashamed, hurt, exhausted, confused and wanting desperately for our lives to be back to our normal interactions. He would always say that I was to blame for his actions and I believed him. I started to see a professional Counselor to try to understand what was wrong and gradually came to understand that he had a problem with his anger. I learned that his father had abused his mother physically and psychologically for years and the children had witnessed it. I now understand that Gary internalized the abuser role and that is what was coming out in our relationship. I realized that even when I did stop doing whatever it was that he said caused him to get so angry and abusive with me he still would find new reasons to explode at me. He was two people: one kind, caring, and gentle and the other rageful and explosive.

This transition from thinking I was to blame for his anger and realizing instead that HE had a problem took about ten years. I began to read about abusive relationships on the sly in the library at the University I worked at and seeing the pattern very clearly in our interactions. I had a bag with clothes in the

house hidden so I could flee from the house at any time if I needed to do so for my safety, which I did do on a few occasions.

I loved him deeply but could not live with the thought of doing that for the rest of my life. I recall sitting on our front porch after walking the dog one warm summer evening and saying to myself "I cannot do this for the rest of life" I heard a voice in my head say "he is going to die." I said it again to myself and heard the same message. I went inside dismayed and wondering what this meant. I said nothing to Gary about it. In October of that year, he was suddenly diagnosed with AIDS. I now believe this was the voice of the Holy Spirit guiding me.

In October of that year, he was diagnosed with AIDS. I thought he had the flu so after five days took him to the doctor who drew blood and announced a day later that he had AIDS. We were quite startled. This was a total shock to me and again I was devastated. I felt determined to continue with my studies but realized I had to learn how to take care of him. So, I read everything I could about the disease and what little was then understood about it (this was in the late 1990's). I realized that I had two choices: to respond with love or to respond with fear. I chose love. I was tested for the virus and found out it had not been transmitted to me. I believe that my Higher Power had protected as we had not practiced safe sex for several years. I stayed with him, taking care of him, until he passed away three years and three months later. Again, my life had fallen apart. I never acquired the disease. AIDS was just being diagnosed and seen in the San Francisco Bay Area. The Center for Disease Control (CDC) was trying to determine how it was transmitted. I recall people did not feel comfortable coming to our house, using the toilet, or eating at our table. I read all I could about the disease and drove down to see my folks. I told them I needed their help and asked it they would help me. My Mom immediately said "of course we will, won't we dear" to my Father. He reluctantly agreed. He was very angry that Gary had done this to me, and I don't blame him. They did come visit for meals.together and supported me as best they could. Thank God for That. Clearly it was not my time to die. He died three years and three months later.

I hope it comes across how much we loved each other. In intimate relationships, our psychological "unfinished business" from childhood and adult trauma comes out. It is the job to then learn how to deal with that in a constructive way. He was not a bad person, he was very wounded. I still love him deeply and now have a better understanding and compassion for how he was suffering inside.

I am sharing this because I hope that if someone is in a similar situation, they will realize similarities and seek help from a professional Counselor, a Battered Women's Shelter or similar resource. I could not change him and only he could if he had wanted to. I understand the confusion of this situation and how others might judge me as naïve for staying with him. But what most people don't understand is how gradually and completely he gained control over my psyche. And the deep love we would return to when these episodes were over.

I have never repeated this pattern again and I think this is because I finally was able to understand it and see it clearly when it was happening again. I now can sense if a man has this emotional makeup in his character and stay away from him.

I should mention that a few days before our wedding I had a very disturbing dream that I was about to marry a man I did not know. I was upset by this but my girlfriend told me it was just jitters and to shake it off. In now realize that it was a warning.

One very healthy way I learned to handle my anxiety when he would get upset was to retreat into the garage and work out on the exercycle. This allowed me to get rid of my adrenaline (fight or flight response). I would ask myself "what am I feeling and what do I want to do about it." This gave me a chance to get centered in myself and come up with a logical plan of action. I highly recommend this to anyone in a stressful situation. I have continued to work out daily (exercycle, treadmill and now walking five miles a day) and it has kept me very healthy.

One day I was asked if I would be willing to do a *pro bono* assessment of the locally funded Batterer's Diversion Program. This was a chance to use my professional skills for the betterment of the community. Leslie and I decided to do this. We met with the Director of the program, gained insight of what they taught, designed a form to collect data on each participant, and went to the jail database to follow-up on the graduates of the program. It took about three months to do all of this. We wrote up the results and were invited to present the results to a group of people. We arrived in the morning to a room full of chairs containing local Police, Parole Officers, Judges, members of the Diversion Program staff and other interested parties. We presented our results which indicated quite clearly that the program was ineffective at permanently changing the behaviors of the male abusers. We noted that there was a high degree recidivism, that is, repeat offences. We further stated that the men were not getting much punishment from the judges in the court. They were oftentimes able to return home after just one night in jail. To our amazement, we watched while a woman Judge turned to the male Judge who presided over that court and asked if this was true. He replied that it was. What we later learned was that he was removed from that court and a woman Judge was put in there who had a zero tolerance for males abusing their wives. The court system was changed locally and has remained so to this day. We were very proud of our efforts on this particular project. We felt that we were able to contribute to the safety of women in our community.

Checklist of Health Issues and Illnesses (CHII)

In the 1980s, my husband was diagnosed with AIDS. This led to a serious inquiry on my part into metaphysical healing. I read a book by Caroline Myss, a Medical Intuitive, called *Why People Don't Heal and How They Can* (1998) [1]. In it she recounted the story of a man, who had AIDS, whom she helped heal by teaching him how to accept his homosexuality and be assertive in life, not feeling ashamed for who he was.

Although Caroline reached this conclusion from working empirically with patients of Dr. Norm Shealy, this concept had already emerged from William James' concept of Healthy-Mindedness. William James was the first to suggest the concept of Healthy-Mindedness in his 1902 book *The Varieties of Religious Experience, Lectures IV and V. The Religion of Healthy-Mindedness.* [2] James describes that "the sort of religious complex ways of experiencing religion and new manners of producing happiness [are the] wonderful inner paths to a supernatural kind of happiness" (p. 26). "We give the name healthy-mindedness to the tendency which looks on all things and sees that they are good" (p. 29). "The great central fact in human life is the coming into a consciousness vital realization of our oneness with this Infinite Life and the opening of ourselves fully to this divine inflow" (p, 33). William

James used this method to heal his lifelong struggle with Depression.

Similarly, in Science of Mind, there is a focus on the positive effects of concentrating on a quality of God that is the opposite of one's mental cause of physical and mental disease (e.g., joy and gratitude would be the opposite of depression and lack). These recommended techniques include prayer, meditation, and Positive Mind Treatment. Various spiritual traditions have grown out of these concepts which were developed by Ernest Holmes. Holmes was influenced by Emma Curtis Hopkins, a well-known spiritualist and "Teacher of Teachers." Her many students went on to make important contributions to the New Thought Movement. One such author was Louise Hays, also born in 1926 or during this period of influential thinkers, who in 1976 wrote a book entitled *Heal Your Body*. [11] In this book she lists issues and attitudes that, when treated by Positive Mind Treatment, can result in healing of the body. This is nearly identical to Caroline's assertion.

These books prompted my interest in going deeper into understanding Subtle Energy. I began attending weekend workshops taught by Caroline Myss and Norm Shealy, M.D., in the late 1990's. My background was in psychometrics, the theory and statistics behind psychological measurement, and one day I proposed to them that I do a research project empirically testing her theory. They agreed and gave me a small grant to do so. This led to the development of a sixty-three item, paper and pencil measure of the attitudes listed in Caroline' book which were also associated with the seven Chakras. Specific items were thought to represent issues for that Charka. For example, hesitations of self-expression related to the Fifth Charka in the throat. Similarly, each Chakra was said to have issues related to it that, which when not dealt with effectively, led to an interruption in the flow of Subtle Energy and a subsequent physical illness also associated with that Charkras, energy vortices bringing in energy to the body from the base of the spine to the top of the hear. The measure was called the Checklist of Health Issues and Illness or CHII. Chi is the Chinese name for Subtle Energy. The Chinese also believe in the importance of the healthy flow of Chi. Tai Chi is a physical practice to promote the flow of Chi. Chinese medicine also treats .illnesses by stimulating energy lines in the body, similarly believing that blocked Chi results in illness.

The CHII was administered to over one thousand workshop participants at one of Caroline and Norm's weekend workshops on healing and Subtle Energy. Participants were believed to be representative of adults in the population in the United States at the time. Sampling restrictions may have including too many females and a socio-economic bias of those who could afford to attend these workshops. An educational bias or self-consciousness bias may also have been present, although a self-awareness was needed to effectively answer the questionnaire. This robust sample allowed for empirical establishment of a Normative Distributions of items within each Chakra using Parametric Statistical Methods. A Frequency Distribution was generated for scores on each Chakra. Caroline posted the measure on her website which allowed further data gathering and for individuals to get their scores on the CHII. They received ratings of "low," "medium" or "high" along with a detailed description of what that score meant, the issues involved in each Chakra. Interested individuals completing the CHII to get personal insight. The next step was to test the relationship between Charka CHII scores and specific illnesses.

I was teaching at the Institute of Transpersonal Psychology in Palo Alto, California at the time and offered a graduate course in research methodologies where the example and task was for students to administer the CHII to specific populations they were interested in. One such example was Massage Therapists giving the CHII to their patients. In this manner, I gathered information on the specific illnesses of the research subjects. I analyzed the magnitude of the relationship (Pearson Corrlation) between illnesses of the research Subjects and their CHII score. The results did not support Caroline's theory. I then did a Factor Analysis to determine if there were underlying concepts which needed to be explored. What I determined, from a Factor Analysis, was that there were three Factors: Relationship to Self, Relationship to Others, and Spirituality as practiced in the individual's daily life. The majority of items loaded on the first two Factors.

When I did the Factor Analysis, I realized that her theory had been oversimplified. Physical healing involved more than specific attitudes, it involved how one related to oneself, to others, and to spirituality. This expanded definition included the concepts of Healthy-Mindedness and Conversion. It also implied that a complete self-acceptance, acceptance of others, and integration of spirituality into one's life was necessary to heal. This made sense to Caroline who concluded that her statements were a bit too simplistic. Nevertheless, great benefit can come from personal self-exploration of attitudes and negative beliefs that impact not only our bodies but also our daily experience of life as well. The results of this inquiry were presented at two professional conferences, one at the International Society for the Study of Subtle Energy and Energy Medicine ISSSEEM in Boulder, Colorado in 1999 and the other at a meeting in San Francisco, California on a panel with Elizabeth Targ on her experience with studying a specialized type of brain cancer. She later developed that cancer and died of it which begs the question did she "attract" the brain cancer to her by her mental and life's energy focus on it? We will never know.

It is still possible that there might be a relationship between illness and the CHII, but further research with a larger sample would be required to answer that question. Several years of workshops, developing and administering the measure, and presenting the results led to my attending Holos Graduate School, teaching Research and Statistics at there, and in 2001 earning a PhD in Integral Energy Medicine.

Meditation

When Gary got diagnosed with AIDS, the Physician assigned to his case asked if we would like to take a meditation class to help handle such a shocking diagnosis. We agreed and went to a several-week long class on Vipassana Meditation of the Buddhist tradition. The introductory pamphlet, developed by a few doctors at the hospital who were studying meditation as explained by Eknath Eshwaran, outlined the benefits of meditation and provided several techniques to try. Eknath Eshwaran was an Indian scholar who taught at a Retreat Center called Spirit Rock in Moonacre, California close to us in Northern California. His book, *The Upanishads,*[3] is a classic text. I decided to memorize a passage from the Upanishads, a spiritual book of Vedic Sanscrit scriptures, still used today in the Hindu Tradition, because I knew my mind liked to keep busy.

There is the passage.
Here O children of immortal bliss!
You were born to be united with the Self.
Follow the path of the illuminated ones
And be united with the Lord of Life. (p. 163)
Hidden in the heart of every creature
Exist the Self, subtler than the subtlest,
Greater and the greatest. They go beyond
All sorrow who extinguish their self-will
And behold the glory of the Self
Through the grace of the Lord of Love. (p. 79)

I started getting up each morning, showering and setting my hair, then meditating at the kitchen table. At first it was for five minutes, repeating the passage and returning my mind to it when it wandered. Later for ten minutes and soon to a half-hour every day. It helped my mind to calm down and for me to feel more centered as I went about my day. That practice has continued off and on for the rest of my life.

Also during my marriage to Gary, I was asked by a dear friend Ardath to join her women's meditation group. It was a small group of dedicated meditators. The task of running the group was passed from participant to participant with each assigned leader choosing rituals from the woven basket of books. We met once a month for at least ten years. In this group, I learned about Pagan Rituals and gained a better understanding of the role of the seasons in our annual cycle of the sun. It was fun to try different techniques such as drumming and Charka meditations. I received wonderful support from this special group of women. Ardath and I are still close friends. She is the one who told me I was like a Phoenix as she has seen me go through many challenges in my life.

Leslie

Leslie was the love of my life. Leslie was a very unique individual. She was extremely intelligent and educated having received a B.A. with distinction in Mathematics and a M.A. in Psychology. She read widely on topics including gardening, spirituality, art, archeology, and anything else that caught her imagination. When she was first a student of mine, she would stop by my office during office hours and we would talk for hours. I would mostly listen to her, because of our respective roles at that time, but I thought to myself that she was telling my story of emotional, psychological, intellectual and spiritual searching and development.

After my husband Gary died, I let myself grieve for his loss. But gradually a desire was welling up in me to be intimate with Leslie on a physical basis. One evening I invited her over for dinner and told her of my desires. I knew that I was not toying with her affection, as I had known for some time that she was in love with me. Now I felt ready to make an emotional commitment to her. She was surprised but delighted to hear of my feelings. And so we began our journey together as lovers and eventually as spouses. We were soul mates.

Before we were together as partners in life we worked together. It was wonderful to be able to discuss with her our many work projects which included gathering data, analyzing it, writing reports, and delivering our conclusions to the appropriate audience of faculty, staff and administrators. As one fellow administrator called us, we were the "dynamic duo."

But mostly it was our home life together that gave me such pleasure and inspiration. With Leslie I was safe in every way. She knew how to handle my emotions and with her I explored heretofore unknown regions of my psyche.

I was finally able to feel safe sexually and to know the desires of my body and their fulfillment. We spent many hours discussing ideas and philosophies. I recall when she moved in with me how many books we had in common. It was amazing. There was no topic off limits.

Leslie was also an artist. She would spend hours drawing with the box of 100 colored pencils I got for her birthday one year, upon her request. She drew landscapes and portraits. Her work was very precise and natural looking. She also enjoyed being creative on the computer and when she retired got great joy out of playing the graphics game called Spore. She would create beings and objects in this imaginary galaxy and often mastered all levels to become "the Master of the Universe" which gave her special creative options. The creatures were joyful and fun.

Leslie was very tender and gentle. But she could also become quite fierce if there were any witnessed transgression by others. She would not shy away from standing up for someone who was being bullied. Her tenderness would guide her to spot gentle souls would needed encouragement in life and she went out of her way to provide nurturance and support for these individuals.

I retired from the University and planned to spend many happy years together with Leslie. But after two years Leslie was diagnosed with cancer. I took care of her as best I could and she fought as hard as she could to stay alive. But on December 27, 2014, she died. I was heartbroken. I did not know how to pick up the pieces of my life this time. I had no work to go to, was aching constantly for her and adrift. We were able to spend twenty blessed years together before she died of cancer. I know that she did not want to leave this earthly plane. After she passed, I was still able to feel close to her and to imagine our conversations together. With her therapist I channeled a communication from her to me from her after her passing. In it she urged me to not kill myself and to go on because it was not my time to leave this earth. As you know, I was devastated with her passing and still feel deep grief at my loss. I know that when I leave this earthly plane we will be together forever and I will know bliss again.

After Leslie died, my alcoholism returned and slowly took over my life.

I was alone, grieving, and desperately trying to find my way. I somehow thought that there would be comfort from the wine I would consume. There was not. Instead it exacerbated my depression and I then experienced two and a half years of insanity. It was my "Dark Night of the Soul."

I was drinking and upset one summer day and called a male friend to come help me. He came over and was comforting me. His wife called and asked what he was doing. She came over and, because she was a nurse at a local hospital and didn't know what to do with me, decided to take me to the Emergency Room. I was very upset that instead of helping me deal with my feelings I was suddenly being handed over to strangers. I was angry at this betrayal of trust.

I then experienced my first 5150 or 72 hour hold. I stayed in the hospital under constant observation, that is, someone was sitting in my hospital room at all times reading a book and just being there. After 24 hours I was transferred to a group room of about eight patients and spent the time working on my computer and calling friends. The Intake Counselor came to interview me after three days and I was no longer suicidal. She had also talked with my counselor, Frances Fuchs, who understood what I was going through as I had started to see her gain. I was let out and returned to my home and life.

To make a long story short, there were a series of suicide attempts, trips in the ambulance, and brief stays in psychiatric hospitals during the next two and a half years. I did not understand what was happening to me. I was an educated accomplished professional woman. I could not come to grips with the fact that I was now being sent from the F.R. to psychiatric hospitals on locked wards. No one was talking to me about what I was experiencing, the fear and dismay. I was given antidepressants and dismissed each time after three days, the time required by law to keep me from harming myself.

I had no idea the havoc alcohol was having on my mind and body. I was given medications for depression and anxiety and taken through detoxification from alcohol, yet no one ever talked to me about alcoholism or the part it was playing in my life. I continued to drink trying to find relief.

But the depression was exacerbated by the alcohol. I attended an out-patient program which helped. However, I knew it was just a matter of time before I would have another suicide attempt.

Finally, on July 7, 2017, I found myself in my living room with my future husband and a kind neighbor saying that I desperately needed help. I had never said that in my entire life, but I knew I was in trouble. I now know that not only did they and the other people I cried out to that day hear my plea but so did my Higher Power. I ended up in the Psychiatric Crisis Unit. At about 2:00 a.m. a male Counselor came into my room in the locked facility to do my Intake Assessment. He asked me if I thought I was an alcoholic. I replied that I did not think so because I always stopped drinking whenever it started to be a problem in my life. He said, quite matter-of-factly, that I was an alcoholic.

Although other people had at times suggested that I stop drinking or expressed concern for me, it was always said with a sense of condemnation and suggestion that I was of "low character." He said it in such a matter-of-fact way, without any condemnation, and it made me curious. I asked him how he could possibly know I was an alcoholic having just met me. He commented on my red face, fat stomach, and the fact that I had an alcohol level of .29 which is way over the legal limit and close to the Black Out level of .30. He also knew my history of hospitalizations. At that time, I did not feel inebriated at all and was surprised to hear that my blood alcohol level was so high. I felt embarrassed and desperate and asked him what I should do. He suggested that I stay at the locked facility on a volunteer basis for two nights, over the weekend, and then return to the Outpatient Program I had successfully completed a few months before. I did that and set as a goal to attend Recovery Meetings to understand alcoholism

Learning About Alcoholism

I walked into a Recovery meeting a week later on a Monday night. When routinely asked in the meeting for new members or someone recently out of a treatment facility, that is, in their first 30 days of sobriety, to introduce themselves, I raised my hand and said that my name was Rose. I was welcomed in such a wonderful way that I felt right at home. After the meeting I went up and asked the woman leading the meeting if she would be my sponsor. She graciously agreed. I then began calling her every day and meeting with her weekly to read the Big Book together and do the Twelve Steps of Recovery.

When I walked into that room, I was totally broken so it was not hard for me to acknowledge that I was powerless over alcohol and that my life had become unmanageable (Step One Appendix A). I did everything that was suggested to me to do. I did the homework assignments suggested by my sponsor and quickly moved through the Twelve Steps. The compulsion to drink was totally removed by my Higher Power. I started to live one day at a time. I experienced a peace and serenity that I had never known. Each day now begins with surrendering my life and will over to a Higher Power and asking that all of my difficulties and limitations be removed so that I may bear witness to the power and love of God. I dedicate myself to do His will always.

I now understand that I was born with a genetic predisposition to alcoholism. I had a grandfather who was said to be an alcoholic. However, I only met him once at the end of his life so did not see any indication of that. I also had an uncle who liked to drink beer and know that he got a DUI once and quit drinking after that. But I rarely saw him and never saw him act inappropriately because of alcohol. But I inherited the gene for alcoholism. Because the disease is chronic and progressive, even when I drank only a few glasses of wine a day, the disease was getting worse. By the time I was drinking heavily after Leslie's death, alcoholism really got a hold of me. I now understand that alcoholism is a disease of the mind, body, emotions and Spirit. Recovery requires healing in all of these four areas. I am definitely in Recovery now. I am so thankful for all of the wonderful people I have met and how they support me daily.

The Third Step Prayer

I just came home from a meeting. Today a woman shared that she was overwhelmed and did not know what to do. She was trying to decide if she should spend her last $10 on a drink. I shared that when I first started, that first night when I got home and was trying to go to sleep, I felt myself falling into that deep depression that I had been battling for two and a half years. I called my sponsor and asked her what to do. She told me to say the Thirds Step Prayer:

"God, I turn my will and my life over to you...to build with me and to do with me as Thou wilt. Relieve me of the bondage of self so that I may do Thy will. Take away my difficulties so that victory over them may bear witness to those I would help of Thy power, Thy Love, and Thy way of life. May I do Thy will always." (page 63 of the Big Book) [9].

I felt the depression lift and have not felt it since that time.

Dreams and Guidance

Shortly after I started to attend Recovery meetings I had a series of three experiences that felt like my Higher Power was communicating to me. The first was a dream I had. In it I was surrounded by a crowd of people who were a little angry and wondering why I was being offered this gift (of sobriety). God was etching into two gold plated tablets the message that I now deserved to have the gift of sobriety because of all that I had been through in this life. The second experience was waking up with the music of a John Lennon song in my head that was conveying to me the deep love that the Creator has for me. The third experience was waking up to the music of Billy Joel in my head saying "You'll be blessed, I promise you that, promise you that…You'll be blessed." I know that my Creator was communicating these thoughts and images to me of reassurance of Its love for me and safety in the process of change that I was experiencing.

Eric

Eric came into my life unexpectedly. I met him one day at a campground that Leslie and I used frequently. We were spending the weekend there celebrating her birthday and invited her two sons and their families to join us. Leslie had helped to raise two twin boys. She was in a relationship with their mother and even though they broke up, she decided to live close by and help raise the boys. She loved them dearly.

One summer day, as we pulled into the campground, a handsome, vibrant, healthy man in his 40's jumped into the RV. I said "hi " calling him by his brother's name. He said "nope, I'm Eric." Thus began our friendship. One of the first things he said was that he liked women without makeup. I thought "how refreshing and what a luxury to live like that."

Eric began to spend time with us, visiting for a few days to be with Leslie. She had cancer then but did not tell Eric. Instead, when we were visiting Leslie while she was in the University of San Francisco Medical Center he realized how sick she was.

Sometime that fall I needed to fly to Oklahoma to take care of Uncle's estate. I had to stay longer than expected and ran out of my medications. By the time I arrived back in Oakland I was getting shaky. Then I made the foolish mistake of drinking when I arrived at the Hilton in Oakland late in the evening because they did not have a workout room I could use to unwind from the trip. I awoke feeling very shaky and realized I could not drive myself back home unless I got the medication necessary to calm my nerves. I called home and asked Eric to please drive all of my medications down to me which he gladly agreed to do. Eric is a loving spirit anxious to please. After several hours (he got lost) he finally arrived. On the way home I asked him if he was gay, because as far as I could tell from his life story he had never had a serious relationship with a woman. Thus began a long conversation about his life. I learned that he was indeed heterosexual and had retreated into a solitary life after a tragic death of his girlfriend the night of the senior prom in high school. He had had a few short relationships, but nothing that lasted a really long time. Instead, he had dedicated himself to a life of surfing in the Santa Barbara area of California while he was working full-time at a grocery store. He did this for 18 years. When I asked him about that he explained it this way:

Have you ever wondered about how the universe works? Have you ever thought "maybe there's an answer you have not been taught in

school?" Eric said to me:

I personally have always been curious and I found my answers in surfing…relating it in nature's power and flow. I learned to watch as waves developed and gradually learned how to "ride" them – that is

– how to connect with nature as it really is. It made me feel small because nature is so big. However, I also felt Love as the guiding force in the Universe. And I tried to listen and follow that voice. It has and is my life's quest.

There have been many problems and challenges along the way as my body got hurt and I could no longer surf "big waves." I have learned to adapt and to find other ways to connect such as music, watching the sunrise and sunset, and so forth. I stop, be still and LISTEN to God's gentle voice speaking through mother nature. I hear birds singing… I hear it in waves crashing… in wind blowing through the trees, and I remember I am not alone. I am a unique, small part of the universe. And just like a symphony takes many instruments tuned and playing together to create the whole, so with life – I am an instrument in the symphony of life.

Eric continued to stay with me off and on after Leslie died. We became very close friends and it was just natural to have him around. One day I realized that I was having sexual feelings toward him. I asked if he felt the same way and said if he did, to simply come downstairs where was sleeping and climb in.One night he did and it was wonderful. We have been together ever since. We were married on May 18, 2017.

Eric is a gentle soul. I love to watch his eyes as they reveal so much about how he is feeling and what he is thinking. We have an easy way together each one being ourselves while relating to each other. He is a tremendous blessing to me.

A New Car

Recently we were returning from taking care Eric's mom home who lives in a county about an hour and a half from here. We were trying to get back in time for me to make the 7:00 pm meeting. Right after we turned off of the freeway and were driving the final two miles to our home, we were rear-ended and pushed into a truck in front of us. The car was totalled

The next morning I went looking for a new car. I found a used Mercedes that I would like to purchase. It feels like it is the right one and that it is God's will taking me into another direction in life. The car has a navigation system that I could use to go to meetings that I've never been to before. I ran the idea by my sponsor before buying it being a little embarrassed at the luxury of it. She said I deserved it and besides, I'd still be the same Rose when I stepped out of it. I agreed. Eric also said that I deserve it.

When I was waiting at the dealership for the paperwork to be drawn up I was walking around by myself. I felt Dad's presence strongly saying "way to go…you have class." He strongly advised me at the end of his life "if you want to do something do it!" I felt comforted by his presence.

A New Book to Read

Tuesday morning, I went to go on my walk as usual. While driving saw a friend from Recovery and turned around to ask if he would like to go on a walk with me. He readily agreed and we had a lovely chat while walking. During our walk he mentioned that Lee in was interested in various philosophies. At the Tuesday night meeting I asked Lee about that. I mentioned the book *Love Without End...Jesus Speaks* by Glenda Green. [10] He then recommended a book entitled *The Disappearance of the Universe* [11] which I came home and ordered. It is about two ascended masters appearing to a man who writes about his conversations just like Glenda Green wrote about her conversation with Jesus when he appeared in her studio and she painted his portrait. I feel like I am being led, day by day, into a new spiritual life. All that is required of me is a willingness to go forward with the intention of being of service to God. It is quite miraculous and also very grounded and simple. I feel very blessed.

I am now reading the book on kindle so can start reading right away rather than waiting two days for the hard copy to arrive (yeah). Here is a quote that seems very important to me:

There is a way to receive *guidance* as to how we are to proceed in the world (pp. 26-27).

Let God have your spirit for it is everything (p. 27).

God's Will

In Recovery we talk a lot about trying to discern and do God's will in our lives. In the book *Love Without End, Jesus Speaks,* by Glenda Green,[10] Jesus explains God's will in this way (pp 314-315):

There are four **levels of intent**…

First is the intent of God. You can summarize the intent of God very sweetly and simply this way. It is LOVE. Love is the will of God…

The second level of intent was placed by the Creator into the physical functions of our universe. This level of intent performs under the power of basically two principles. One is that life and the living shall prevail over the dead and the dying. That is the will of God, so whenever you support life and the living, you are in harmony with the will of God for this universe. The other principle which resides under this intent for physical well-being is the law of cause and effect (note Hindu concept of karma). The Creator intends for the universe to return always to a state of balance. No matter how far a state of existence might swing to 'the left' it will always be rebalanced to 'the right' and eventually back to center…

The third aspect of intent relates to the subject of respect and justice within the brotherhood of man. You do not live alone. You live within a family, a brotherhood, and the plan is that someday it will be a wonderful brotherhood…

Then last though by no means least, are your own intentions, if you are intent and understand what you have set in motion.

These seeds you planted, possibly a long time ago, and are still growing…

It is hard to know what these intents are because they were planted as seeds in our brain and heart at an early age and they shape how we define and experience this physical reality. It takes a lot of soul-searching and reflection to get to the origin of these assumptions and intents and psychotherapy, prayer, and talking to a trusted person can help us in this regard.

The Sacred Heart

According to Jesus (as found in *Jesus Speaks: Love Without End*) At the center of your soul is the Sacred Heart. This is the point at which you are one with God. The heart sees infinity within and without. It can behold perfection. And it can ascertain the origin of conditions and change them. The heart is your higher intelligence. (p. 49)

Your mind is merely a servant, and it behaves well if it is given positive impulses: It behaves very poorly if it is given negative impulses. (p. 50)

This advice is also given by Hindu gurus who simply state that the mind is a wonderful servant but a terrible master.) Similarly, in Taoist teachings the mind and heart are not separate but rather referred to as "the heart-mind."

What Western emphasis on the mind has meant to me in my life is that for 32 years I believed that the way to "truth", of the understanding of the Universe, was through the mind. So I spent that time in higher education getting an EdD in Quantitative Methods in Educational Psychology from the University of California at Berkeley. I described my own personal experience of studying statistics and auantitative methods in educational psychology as climbing a tree. At the first course, Introduction to Statistics taught to me in a Master's program, is the trunk of the tree: The bottom and largest part of the discipline. And as I progressed with each additional course over the period of ten years I felt like I was climbing up that tree then onto a limb and eventually at the very end of the limb I fell into the hands of God. I realized that,although statistics can explain a lot about what is happening in our world, when we apply the correct data in the scientifically driven way, it does have limits. That is when I turned, once again, to the spiritual realm to try to understand truth.

I began attending workshops, during the weekends, taught by Drs. Norm Shealy and Caroline Myss. I gained a new understanding of the workings of the universe and our lives. I studied the metaphysical and alternative methods of healing from Drs. Norm Shealy and Caroline Myss. After a few years I received a PhD in Alternative Methods of healing. All of this has been my personal journey to understand the universe and I share it with you now in case you find it meaningful or helpful in your life. We live in a pivotal time and it is important to do all we can to discern how to relate to the Divine Principles of the Universe, by whatever name you give it.

Once again I quote from Glenda Green's book: …The answers to healing your life will be found in the inner strength of your heart…I give you three practices: The first is to strengthen all of your positive emotions through daily gratitude and admiration of the beautiful world around us. The second is to disempower your negative emotions daily through forgiveness. The third practice you will have to work at a little more diligently, …What I am referring to is "innocent perception" (p. 51)

Innocent perception is a way of looking at the world without judgment. Most of us, when we see something, are making judgments about it (what a beautiful sunset, what a messy room, etc.) Jesus suggests that we simply observe the world as it is. The heart is your connecting link to God and the universe, which integrates your own unique center of experience, awareness, and character with that which is beyond your comprehension…The heart is magnetic, silent, and still. The feeling of being there is like one of resting in a peaceful Heavenly lake, or floating in a vacuous space. As a magnetic center, your heart is the generator of all your life energy, and whenever you empower your heart you raise your energy level physically, mentally, emotionally, and spiritually. Within the heart you will also find clarity, resolve, steadfastness, intent, stillness, respect, justice, kindness, and perceptions of greatness. (p., 155)

Depression

I never understood depression until I had it. It was about two and a half years after Leslie had passed. I was grieving but trying to handle life. Then on Memorial Day 2016 I was watching TV in the TV room upstairs and I heard a dripping noise. I walked downstairs and realized that water was dripping from the ceiling onto the floor in the dressing room. I put a trash can under the drip and called Eric asking him to come home and help me. I realized that the entire rug area of the dressing room was wet and there was a big problem.

To make a long story short, I called a plumber and he came out. It was expensive because it was the Memorial Day weekend. The plumber was able to assess some of the damage and replace the water heater.

However, that began a six-month project to deal with the damage that had been done to the house. Eventually we had to remove everything from every room in the house (except my office which I refused to do) out onto the lawn in the back yard. The entire house had to be painted on the inside, the carpets replaced and the flooring in the kitchen and two bathrooms replaced. While this was being done, we had to move out and stay in hotels for about three weeks while asbestos was removed and humidifiers were run 24 hours a day for several days. I felt like everything I had worked for during the past 30 years was ruined. This began a huge depression for me. (Now I see it was a blessing as it helped me create a new feeling in our home and get rid of a lot of stuff of Leslie's that I had not taken care of. But that is now.)

I felt totally overwhelmed and did not know how I was going to pay for all of this. We filed a claim with my State Farm home owner's policy, but that involved many conversations and visits with representatives from State

Farm and the many contractors that we involved in fixing the problems. My computer was disconnected and I lost the ability to do my on-line banking and hired a fiduciary to handle my finances. I went from being a competent Associate Vice President to what felt like a bumbling idiot. Although I was not drinking alcohol at the time, I gradually fell deeper and deeper into a depression. I felt hopeless that life would ever feel good again. Eventually I tried to kill myself by cutting my own throat with a razor blade. I figured that Eric would be better off without me so I arranged things so he would have the finances he needed to get by, drove my car out to a road away from our house, layed in the back seat and cut my throat. Surprisingly it did not hurt. It was wet as the blood drained down my neck and onto my shoulders but not painful. I sliced many times and waited to pass out. But I didn't pass out and just heard cars passing by. I got bored and decided to drive home. I arrived home and as I walked toward Eric he realized I was bloody and got alarmed. He asked what had happened and I told him. He called 911 and an ambulance and the police came. I was loaded into the ambulance and the EMT said "no one is going to die on my watch." I thought he was being ridiculous and that I would not die if my body stopped functioning but would simply leave it and my sprit would float away, which is what I wanted. I was taken to a hospital, given emergency surgery (as I had nearly cut the caratid artery) and after a few days moved to a psychiatric hospital. I was given antidepressants and sent home. But the depression did not lift and I then spent eighteen months in hell until I finally got into Recovery. I did get some relief from the Outpatient Program but, as you know, started drinking after the first try at the program and had to return after my intake with Todd at the Crisis Stabilization Unit on July 7, 2017.

 What made me think about all of this is that last Friday, the day I bought the Mercedes, when I was coming home from the Recovery meeting I realized I felt happy for the first time in a very long time. I had been at peace, but this was happiness which is different. I have during the past few days gradually come back to this life. I have my sexuality back and a joy of living. I have started writing in this journal which I hope to turn into a book. I feel empowered in all ways and manage my own finances (and have since June but that is another story). I am even using the turn signals on my car which I had stopped doing feeling quite content to die in a car crash. I had not realized how totally I had withdrawn from life until I was coming back into it. I am even reading an exciting book when I go out to eat by myself so feel that I am back to normal. I am calling friends and just arranged to meet my sister for our traditional Christmas high tea together. I realize now that I have been withdrawing from the world for eighteen months and that is a very long time. Thank God I am back! Amen

I am in awe at how wonderfully my life continues to grow day by day and I work the Recovery program and turn my life over to God. Just a year ago I was in a psychiatric hospital and my jeweler graciously cashed in some gold coins I had from Mom and Dad and offered to let me stay in the unit behind her house that she had built for her mother to stay in when she visited. You cannot buy that kind of kindness for any amount of money. It was simply the result of years of my coming into her store, talking, and buying things (or selling old wedding rings) and our friendship naturally grew out of those encounters. I am happy to bring her business. She also gave us a Christmas basket full of goodies which is our first gift this year. Eric has been buying poinsettias for the house and it feels so festive. I had needed to do Christmas differently this year so as to not be reminded of how Leslie and I used to do it. I called my sister and we agreed to meet for Christmas tea which we have done for many years. And a friend who returned my call after I left her a message asking if she would care to meet for lunch. She was so enthusiastic and welcoming. I'll meet her on Tuesday next week and my sister on Thursday next week. I am gradually

returning to be a participant in this world in a sober and grounded way. Life is beautiful and so blessed!

Higher Power

I now understand my Higher Power to be the voice of Christ or the Holy Spirit (the same thing) that is contrasted to the voice of the ego. I now ask that Christ or Jeshua (his name in Aramaic) be what I listen to throughout the day (and night). After reading *Disappearance of the Universe* [11] I understand the purpose of life to be an opportunity to remember God and that I am not separate (really) from God. I understand God to be a state of perfection and love, constant and forever unchanging.

This God consciousness is what I was headed toward when I fell and hit my head on a rock when I was 17. My consciousness left my body and I floated toward a bright light and a feeling of wonderful unconditional love that I had not, until that time, known. That is where I will return to when I eventually finish thinking I am separated from God and return home. In the meantime, I am practicing listening to the voice of Jeshua and feeling peace and serenity and forgiveness for myself and everyone in the world. I don't remember this often and still have more to read in the book and then to practice forgiveness as I do the *Course in Miracles* but at this moment it all seems so clear and simple. It is not easy, but simple.

Spiritual School

It is now 2018 and I continue to grow in Spirit. I have realized recently that, in spite of what I may be doing physically in this world (going to meetings, walking around Spring Lake with Eric, seeing my sponsor…) internally I am aware that there are two voices: the voice of the ego and the voice of Spirit. I, the observer, watches as my awareness goes between these two sources. The ego side gets upset about things that happen, wants to control other people and the outcomes of things, and so forth. The Spirit voice is calm and constant, detached yet loving, free of concerns about the outcome of events in this world

I just came from see Frances, my therapist, and discussing this shift in consciousness. She pointed out that it has taken Leslie leaving this world for me to search for Spirit. It is a positive way of viewing Leslie's passing. Without it I would not have fallen into deep despair and alcoholism and that led me to being open to accept that I am an alcoholic and am now on a spiritual path. As I explain it now, I attend Recovery meetings six days a week and I see it as going to spiritual school. I am learning more each day and am among other people who are also in spiritual school and earnestly trying to apply spiritual principles to their lives. We are not perfect, but we are trying. I now see that whenever I reached toward something external to myself that was not Spirit (statistics, career, Leslie) I was staying stuck in this world. Now I am reaching out to Spirit which is not of this world but within and without it. This is a dramatic shift.

2017 in Review

In reviewing 2017 I realize that it was a very pivotal year for me. I got into Recovery which is a blessing and a total life-style change. I feel peace and serenity most of the time. I got married to Eric. The people who were most influential were Todd, the Intake Counselor at the Crisis Unit who told me I was an alcoholic; Matt, the Counselor at the Out Patient Program who helped me transition into Recovery; and my Sponsor in Recovery. Frances, my therapist, has also been a wonderful ally and guide for me during this time. I will continue to see her. On December 27, 2017 it was the third year since my dear Leslie's transitioned to the other side. I know we are together in Mind, but I still miss talking with her and having her to relate to.

In terms of 2018, I don't have any great changes planned. I want to continue in the life-style I have created which is very health oriented physically, emotionally, and spiritually.

I just came from having lunch alone, because Eric was sleeping in, and read in *The Disappearance of the Universe*. I am almost finished with this book. It stated that we die when we have learned the lessons we came to learn in this lifetime. That makes sense to me.

I am also now doing *A Course in Miracles* [12] each day. Today's thought is that I am here to forgive as my function as a bringer of light into this world and when I fulfill this function I am happy. That is a wonderful thought to ponder and apply today.

Yesterday we drove north to the county his mom lives in to let his mom's care giver know that she is no longer needed. We found someone who is experienced in dealing with Alzheimer's and death and is very easy to work with. She is energetic and responsive to suggestions regarding his mom's care such as taking her outside for walks and to the movies when it is sunny and she is up for it. I know this is the right decision for her. She is sad to see her other care giver go but Eric and I are quite relieved. The previous care giver lied to us and created much turmoil in our lives. I hope that she finds the help she needs to become a healthy, functioning adult. I bless her and have asked repeatedly that I change. I was shown gradually and consistently that she was not right and that it was time to replace her.

And that has now been accomplished.

That's all I have to write today. It is rainy today I walked my five miles around Spring Lake as usual, went out to lunch at our favorite local restaurant and am now doing things until I leave for the Recovery meeting tonight. There is a new woman who has asked for a ride sometimes to meetings so I will check with her and see if she wants to go tonight. I feel so blessed with my new life.

Dreams, Being Broken, and Blackouts

I awoke to the following dream this morning:

I am a male "priest", a younger man, being recognized as earning the right to perform a ritual of "achievement", having arrived. There was gold in our head caps. An older male and another priest were there instructing me in how to perform this ritual. I was being "initiated"

I have realized that a prerequisite to being ready to accept what Recovery has to offer is being "broken", that is, realizing deep in one's soul that all of our efforts to handle our life and solve the riddle of how to live a

"comfortable" life have failed. One is then ready to finally, without reservation, ask for help – from other people and from a Higher Power (weather we realize we are asking at that level or not). This is the prerequisite to taking/experiencing the first step: Admitted we were powerless over alcohol, that our lives had become unmanageable.

Those who enter Recovery before this "opening" don't get it and don't stay. Those who are here are ready to begin the process.

I now realize that I had black outs – times when I would "awake" and realized that I was in conversations with others and did not remember what happening before that. I can be quite startling.

Alcoholism is "a physical craving combined with a mental obsession" (from the Big Book) [9]. Yes I remember physically feeling the desire to consumed wine so that I would physically feel "ok" – even for a little while. The mental obsession was the constant awareness that I "needed" to have alcohol available – e.g., when I arrived to stay at a friend's house on vacation or when travelling on business, knowing that I had my small bottle of gin in my cosmetic bag so that after I landed at the hotel, had put my clothes into the drawers, and worked out, that I could relax with a gin and talk with Leslie about our days.

The change now is that I don't expect any chemical to be able to change my mental state (except antidepressants but they are not a way to "get high" only a way to keep from plummeting down into the depths of depression. I now need to work with whatever psychological state I'm in to get out of it, that is, to accept what it is, honor it, sit with in, and see what to do next about it. Sometimes the only thing to do is to keep following my normal routine of walking five miles in the morning, go out to lunch, and go to a Recovery meeting in the evening. Now that we are spending both Saturday and Sunday driving up north to take care of Eric's mom, our time for fun had changed. I realized I was missing our drives on Highway 1 up to three hours for dinner and then drive back. So we did that last Thursday instead of going to a meeting that night. It was fun and I realized while driving that I really have grown used to having that time to relax and let my mind wander and to talk with Eric. The depression that I felt so deeply last Monday when I saw Frances has passed by doing these things. I'd like to remember this in case that feeling returns someday.

Message From Leslie

Yesterday I was cleaning my office and found the message from Leslie after she passed. Shortly after Leslie passed, I went to see Frances, who was also Leslie's therapist. I was telling Frances that I felt so close to Leslie as though she was sitting right next to me. I felt that Leslie had something to tell me. Frances said she would write down what I felt that Leslie was saying and this is what she channeled to me:

"Oh Sweetheart, take care of yourself, don't hurt yourself. Please don't feel bad, please forgive yourself – I do.

I know I was a burden and it was a hard load to carry.

So sweetheart please don't kill yourself. We are still together.

I'm so sorry I had to die, I didn't want to die. I never meant to leave you and know in your heart I never will leave you – you can always call on me for support and love. Read your card and try, try to see the awe in the world, the beauty.

It's not your time. You have more to do, more to offer. Write your book, it will help people. They will want to read it.

My sons need you too."

As I read this message today, I realize Leslie was talking about this book not the one I was working on then that has been incorporated into this one. I do feel that this journal has depth and deals with some of life's hardest issues to reconcile.

Death

I used to believe we had to get ill before our spirit could leave our body. I now realize that is not so. When our time on earth is finished, when we have finished learning the lessons we came to learn in this life, we die. That is true whether one has lived a few moments or many years.

When I was in college, I studied the Martial Art of Kodenkan Ju Jitsu and earned a Black Belt. It happened that the head of the system, the 10th Dan (Black Belt) also lived there. I was fortunate to study under him for several years. He taught healing arts along with the throws and holds that we learned. His philosophy was that whatever damage we were able to do to someone, we could also heal.

One summer he started spending special alone time with each of us students with whom he had a special relationship. I used to go along with him in the evenings after his work as he visited people who had asked him to come by and heal them. He never charged for this. One day he gave me the book *Three Magic Words* which is about the fact that our life will reflect what we believe to be true.

One day he asked me to drive him down to the Oakland airport to catch a plane back to New York. He was going to some Ju Jitsu event that several of the leaders of the system would be attending. His plane left very early in the morning and he wanted me to drive him down, which I did. After I left him at the gate, I headed for the restroom. While in there I "heard" his voice in my head saying "I am going to die in New York." I was startled and then I heard it again. I did not know what to do with that knowledge, but simply forgot it and drove home. That was on a Saturday morning. On that Sunday

I received a call telling me that he has died the night before while the group was out to dinner and he had choked on a piece of steak. Clearly, he knew that his time on earth was ending.

After he died, I had a series of three dreams about him. He came to me to comfort me as I was missing him deeply. I have noticed that often in my life when a major transition is about to occur, I will have a series of three dreams preparing me for those changed. In the final dream he told me that he needed to move on and that if I really needed him, he would come to help me. I did not need him again and never dreamt of him again.

When I was 16, I was standing in the atrium of our family's home while my Mother sewed some fabric onto my leotard for a modern dance performance at my high school. It was hot and I fainted and hit my head on a rock. What I experienced what floating out of my body, being on my back with my feet forward, in a totally dark area. I gradually began to move forward toward a speck of white light ahead. As I moved toward the light I felt an unconditional love that I had never felt before. It was

wonderful and I thought "this is home and I want to go there." Then I heard my Mom and sister calling my name and thought "oh darn, I have to go see what they want." I then woke upon on the living room couch surrounded by my Mom, sister, and the family doctor who said I had fainted and was now fine. I never told anyone about what I had experienced for I realized it was not something anyone ever talked about. Years later I was working at Tower Records in Chico putting myself through college. I worked in the book section and ran across the book about Near Death Experiences by Raymond Moody. As I read it I realized that was exactly what I had experienced. Since then I have never been afraid of death

A Progressive Disease

Alcoholism is a progressive disease. What does this mean? I heard a good explanation at a meeting the other day. Imagine your life as being a horizontal line. You move along it as you live your life. Then you start drinking alcohol. That is another line that starts to slope downward. You continue with drinking until you experience some negative consequences and then you stop drinking and return to your horizontal life line. Even when you have stopped consuming alcohol, the alcohol line continues to drop downwards so that, if you relapse and start drinking again, you will return at a worse point than when you stopped. That means that the negative consequences will happen sooner than before. Alcoholism is fatal if left untreated. That means that you will die if you do not stop drinking (if you are an alcoholic). I hear stories in meetings of someone (I don't know as of now) who was in the meetings but went out and died. This is very sad.

Fear

One of the things that we have to look at in ourselves as we go through the twelve steps is our fears. Recently I was explaining this to my sponsee and gave her an example I had written down when I was working on that step. I stated I had the fear that my life would have no meaning and that I had so many years ahead to live on this earth. It caused me to seek meaning through volunteer work which never panned our for one reason or another. I said, however, that I no longer had that fear because I have turned my will and life over to my Higher Power and trust that I will be guided to how I might be of service.

I came home and forgot about that conversation when the phone rang. It was from someone I did not know at a publishing company that was interested in promoting my first book, which was rather technical in nature related to my career in Higher Education. I said that I did not want to promote that one, but would be interested in promoting the one I was working on now that was rather metaphysical in nature. I asked him to call me back in three months to check on my progress. He said they would be happy to publish it. I though how amazing! I gave up having anything happen and my Higher Power took over and brought this person into my life. I think it is meant to happen and this pleases me to think I can be of service to others.

The Rhythm of My Week

Every morning, except Saturday, I get up at 9:00 a.m. and drive to a half hour to a beautiful park. Then I walk for five miles around the lake, which takes about two hours. Then I drive up, shower and change and Eric and I go out for breakfast. Eric comes with me on the walks except when he is ill, which he has been for about the last month, with the flue and a virus. Mondays I then go and see Frances, my therapist, at 2:00.

Then I usually get my car washed at the Mercedes dealership on the way home. That gives me a break of a few hours to watch the PBS News Hour and do whatever else needs to be done. I then go to the evening Recovery meeting which starts at 7:00. I like to get there about 20 minutes early to remind myself why I'm there and touch base with my friends in the program. Monday night is a Newcomer's meeting which is fun because while the speaker is sharing their story, we pass around a list for people to write their questions. It leads to a lively discussion. Tuesday is the same schedule but I see my sponsee rather than Frances. Tuesday night is a book study which is interesting as we read and discuss the first 644 pages of the big book. Wednesday is open in the afternoon so we sometimes go to the cinema to catch a movie. Wednesday night meeting has its own flavor and I like to attend it. Thursday is our fun day. After lunch we drive on the coast highway which takes about three hours. I enjoy driving and listening to the music. It's also a chance to space out and think about things. We then go to dinner and return home in time to go to bed. Friday we drive out to the coast for dinner before the meeting. A friend from the Tuesday night meeting works there and it is fun to see her. Saturday mornin,g I meet with my sponsor and attend an 11:00 – 12:30 meeting. After a bit to eat, we drive up to see Eric's mom. She needs in-home care and we have a great person during the week, but Eric and I do it on Saturday and Sunday

We visit her for a while, drive to a local restaurant for dinner, then bring her a hot meal and come home. Sunday after my walk and lunch, we go up again as do the same thing, except before we leave we go shopping at Safeway so she has lots of good food to eat during the week. So this is my rhythm of the week which I find pleasant and fulfilling at the same time.

Bless Her and Change Me

My sponsor has taught me that when I am having trouble with someone, that is, when their behavior upsets me, to bless them and pray that I be changed. This didn't make much sense until I applied it to my mother-in-law's caregiver who was driving me crazy. I tried many different times to get her to understand what we wanted her to do to take care of my mother-in-law. She takes care of her Monday through Friday and we take care of her Saturday and Sundays. Because we rarely saw each other, being there at different times, I tried making a list of what we wanted her to do, creating menus, and leaving a cookbook to reference, using the food that we would buy Sunday nights. We asked her to start a log of what food was prepared and what my mother-in-law ate so we could know that she was getting nutritious meals. This went on for several weeks and it seemed to me that her caregiver was not really understanding what we needed. So we drove up on a Friday unexpectedly to have a face- to-face conversation We explained that my mother-in-law's needs were changing as alzheimers was setting in and that we needed to be clear on what she was doing to take care of the things we expected. Fine, we had agreed and I felt hopeful. One thing the caregiver said was that she was there the five and a half hours per day Monday through Friday and if, for some reason she could not make it over, she would call us to let us know so we could go up. Well the next Monday we called to see if she had arrived at 1:00 in the afternoon, as agreed upon, and the caregiver had not arrived.

We called for the next several hours and realized that she was not coming, so we told Eric's mom to take her meds and fix herself some food to eat. Then we drove up on Tuesday to talk with the caregiver. When we arrived, the caregiver had just put in the pot roast with carrots, potatoes and onions as I had prepared it to stick into the oven. We discussed the fact that she was not here Monday and the conversation turned heated as she tried to deny that fact. When I realized that the caregiver had put on the food log that Eric's mom had eaten half of the pot roast that was only then being cooked, I said that was a lie. The caregiver said she had gotten confused in writing that down and a heated conversation continued. To make a long story short, we ended having to go up four days in one week. Eric and I were at our wits end. All this time I had been blessing her and praying for me to change. When we were on the way home from the third trip of that week, I realized that I was upset and the caregiver was not. I finally realized I could not continue to live with this situation. I went to the county agency in charge of In Home Support Services and asked for a list of available caregivers. I interviewed a few on the phone the next day and arranged to meet one, who looked promising, that coming Sunday.

We met her and signed her up. We then had to drive up on Monday to let the old caregiver know that her services were no longer needed. Which we did. She was upset but our minds were made up. I hope she learned something from the whole episode as I certainly had. So I was finally able to let go and let God work out a situation that I had tried fervently and ineffectively to change.

So now when I am upset with someone in my life, I realize pretty quickly that I need to pray for them and ask God to change me. I strongly recommend this to everyone.

Hope and Joy

I have spent so much time taking about the difficulties in life and realize that now, after seven plus months of sobriety, that my life is full of hope and joy. Where I used to be so depressed that I wanted to kill myself, I know feel hope each morning as I say my Third Step and Seventh Step Prayers and turn my will and my life over to God. I have hope that I will be able to be a blessing to those in my life that day and meditate to ask that I hear the voice of my Higher Power that day. Each day in spent in conscious awareness of my Higher Power. Sometimes I get upset by unexpected occurrences, but I quickly realize I am off balance and apply a tool from the program to get me recentered.

I also experience joy in unexpected moments. I love to drive my new car up the coast along the highway listening to music and relaxing. I feel joy when I sit at the table with Eric eating a meal and marveling that we find new things to talk about and share every day. We laugh a lot together. Life is easy and full.

So I want to be clear that sobriety is not just being serious. In fact I laugh a lot at the Recovery meetings. Everyone there is there by choice to learn about how to life a sober life and help others along the way. It is awe inspiring to me that we can come together to share our common desire to live a God-centered life and be so open and real with each other. Here is no room for pretense. Everyone expects absolute honesty and that's what we get. Of course, not everyone is into Recovery and we oftentimes have newcomers which is wonderful because I can remember my first day walking in, feeling ashamed and uncertain, and want to extend to the newcomer the welcoming had and warm embrace that I received.

Suicidal Thoughts

It is not uncommon for a person sharing their story at a meeting for them to mention that, before Recovery, they had suicidal thoughts. This is partly because alcohol is a depressant so it creates a dark and depressed mood in the person who consumes it regularly. The other reason is that by the time a person ends up in Recovery they are spiritually bankrupt. What this means is that they have tried to use alcohol as a way to solve problems in their lives and that does not work and generally creates more havoc the longer one turned to it as an answer. The alcoholic usually knows, but the times they get to Recovery, that they have a problem and may even suspect that they are alcoholic. The craving to consume alcohol in the face of increasing negative consequences and the inability to stop is seen as an example of the type of insane thinking that is typical of an alcoholic.

Last night a man shared his story of how he ended up in Recovery. He said that after he had a relapse after being sober for a year he realized that he had two choices: go back to Recovery or kill himself. He said that was not an easy choice to make. Fortunately for him, and us, he go back into Recovery and had nine years of sobriety. But many people do not make it back.

Another woman shared her story. She was drinking alcoholically every day and as she drove to work she passed over a bridge. She found herself thinking "is today the day I drive off the bridge?'

It is hard to describe the depths of despair and self-loathing that can be present in an alcoholic before they get into Recovery. It is confusing and alarming at the same time. Because it is a disease that is progressive and fatal, if not treated, things just keep getting worse for the individual who has passed over that line of being able to control drinking. For me, I would start out saying I'd just have two drinks at dinner and within a few months I would end up in crisis and another trip to the ER. Still I did not understand what was happening to me. Thank God I now know. For some people, they pass over that line with the first drink in childhood or early adulthood. For me, I drank for 40 years before I finally got to Recovery. But I crossed that line way before I got to Recovery. I just didn't realize it.

One of the reasons I am writing this book is the hope that someone might read it and realize some similarities with their own life and get help. That is why I am being so honest and self-revealing. Honesty is part of what is also required to recover from alcohol addiction. That and a willingness to do "whatever it takes" to recover. What that entails will be discussed further as we go on.

You Don't Do It Alone

Recovery is a "we" program, not an "I" program. You don't do it alone. You read the Big Book and do the steps with a sponsor (although you can, of course, read on your own). And the meetings are with other people so want to help you to learn to learn to love yourself and to understand the program of Recovery. Most meetings end with everyone in a circle holding hands with the statement that we do not do this alone and in support of the alcoholic who still suffers. Then the Lord's Prayer is usually said.

But, to be clear, this is not a "Christian" program, it is available to anyone no matter what denomination or religion you may ascribe to or even if you are an atheist or agnostic. It is a spiritual program with reliance on a power greater than yourself. For some people that is the group of other alcoholics who are present at the meeting. Each person comes to a person understanding of a power greater than themselves in their own way. What is nonnegotiable is that it is not YOU. On our own we cannot stop alcoholism. That is clear to anyone who has experienced this disease.

Being Secretary

The Secretary is the person who runs the Recovery meetings. They are elected by the group to a six-month commitment and you need to have six months sobriety to be eligible. I now have seven months sobriety. The Secretary usually switches between being a woman and a man. At the Monday night newcomer's meeting, the current Secretary just announced that his term will be over at the end of this month. Ron, one of the Recovery members, asked if I would be willing to be the next Secretary. I said I would. He will nominate me at next Monday's meeting and then it will be my turn to be the Secretary. I'll keep notes here of what that is like for me.

Last night I was voted in as the new Secretary at the Monday night meeting. I feel so blessed and glad to be of service in this way. It feels like a vote of confidence by the other members that I am on track in the program. I spent the afternoon calling women from the phone lists I've gotten at meetings setting up for them to come share their story at the Monday night meeting. We'll see how this all unfolds according to God's will.

It's Wednesday and I have been calling women to see if they are available and willing to share their story at one of our Monday night meetings. It is really fun. I am going from a phone list I got from that meeting. Many of the women listed I don't know if I've met them or not, such is the anonymity of Recovery. What I am struck by is, for those I do ready, how pleasant and willing they are. It's an uplifting experience.

H & I

H & I stands for Hospitals and Institutions. At the Saturday morning meeting my coffee commitment ran out and a woman at the meeting nominated me for the H & I position. I accepted. I know that it requires that I announce at each meeting what H and I stands for and ask for people's spare change for the program. Next Wednesday evening I go to attend my first orientation to find out what else it might entail. I know that for me, I could have benefitted from someone talking to me about alcoholism when I was hospitalized. So it would be a pleasure to be able to do that for another person. I'll keep notes here about what it is like for me do to this commitment.

Last night at the Monday night meeting the speaker was wonderful and inspiring. She mentioned that during several hospitalizations for alcohol related effects she was never talked to about alcoholism. I went up after the meeting and mentioned that had happened to me and that I was now going to be active in the Hospitals and Institutions service. She said she was also and we should see each other Wednesday evening when I go for me orientation and the monthly meeting. I am looking forward to being of service in this capacity.

I just returned from the Wednesday night orientation and monthly meeting. It didn't feel right for me to be involved at this level now. Most positions require on year sobriety, which I don't have. Basically I felt overwhelmed by the number of people there, about 200. I am an introvert and prefer a smaller venue. I will fulfill my six-month commitment to H & I and see if I feel drawn to this line of service at a later time.

It's My Disease Talking

In meetings I often hear people sharing that "it is my disease talking," I have come to understand what they mean. There seems to be a part of my mind that remembers drinking as a "way out" of emotional turmoil and it sits on my shoulder always waiting for an opportunity to talk to me and take over, even though that is not true for me now.

Yesterday was a perfect example. It was a typical Saturday and was going well. I met my sponsor, talked about making an amends I'm working on, stayed for the meeting and then came home. I felt unsettled about the amends I'm working on. It's hard to stay focused on what I want to say, that I am sorry for times my illness may have hurt them. Instea,d I find myself feeling ashamed or afraid of some negative thing the person might say to me. Well, I picked up Eric and we headed up North to check on his mom. I relaxed a bit listening to the music in the car. But when we got there, there was a notice that her rent check had bounced which was a total surprise. The prompted Eric to get upset about that and the fact that his replacement cell phone, from the one that he misplaced, did not have the bank ap on it so he was not able to check her balance, and there we were, off center again. We tried to problem solve but the conversation seemed to fall back onto anger which I knew was not a helpful response.

While we were at dinner, I said that I just needed to be quite for a while and find my center again. The problem was that I wasn't finding it.

Instead I was seeing people around me in the restaurant and bar drinking and looking relaxed and I thought "well if I could just have a drink I'd be o.k" Of course I know this was an idiotic idea.

Then I thought back in my mind to the recent times when I started to think that, let myself have two glasses of wine at dinner, and a few months later would end up in the ER because of alcoholism. It's an insidious process where I have a drink, feel that craving again, and start planning when I can have the next drink. That leads to an obsession of mind where I start planning when I can buy wine, where I can keep it out of sight, how I can sneak drinks, and the insanity that that leads to.

Fortunately I remember that for me now, having a drink is not simply having a drink. It's giving way to the insanity of alcoholism. It is my disease talking to me.

Well the day ended up being a struggle for me listening to these two sides of my mind. I did manage to NOT take a drink, which is step

number one. I found myself thinking "do I really believe in this God stuff? Am I just fooling myself?" That didn't help any. So I'd say a little prayer, asking for help, and that helped me for a few minutes. I tried making a gratitude list in my mind and realized how much I have to be grateful for today. But that normal peace of mind that I have was gone and wasn't coming back. I finally resolved to just get home and go to bed, which I did. I gratefully crawled into bed and went to sleep.

Today I awoke rested and calm again I was able to sleep in and gently enter the day I said my third step prayer and seventh step prayer and talked and "listened" to God for a while in my mind. I realized it was a perfect time to write another chapter in my book on this topic.

So for today, I am recentered, at this moment any way. It's time to head up North again to deal with the unfinished business of the bounced check and whatever else the day may bring. But I do so, knowing in my heart and mind that I am not doing it alone which makes me cry tears of gratitude as I type this. I am so thankful for my sobriety.

Similarities Not Differences

It is often said that we should look for similarities not differences between us as we hear people share their stories. This is because we each have a unique journey that we travel to get into the rooms of Recovery. Alcoholism does not discriminate on demographics such as race, ethnicity, socioeconomic status, sexual orientation, age, or gender. It is a disease that can strike anyone.

The variety of stories heard in Recovery is amazing. Hearing another's life story and journey into Recovery can be very humbling. I realize how sheltered and limited my life experiences are compared to others. Perhaps it is because we live in a city with close approximation to a state prison that I hear stories of people who have been in jail and prison. Theirs is often the story of coming from a home that knew addiction of all kinds. I hear men and women who, from an early age such as 11, describe how they used drugs to alter their reality. It is not unusual for them to get into trouble with the law and end up in Recovery by the age of 20. It is also common to hear of many attempts to get sober, of being in and out of treatment centers before Recovery finally "stuck". I hear these stories and am in awe of that person's tenacity, their ability to keep going in spite of all the hardships life has brought to them. As I have talked about elsewhere, it is not uncommon for someone to be at a crossroads between suicide and Recovery so bleak the desperation and isolation of alcoholism can be. This seems to be a necessary component to the willingness to cry out in all honesty for God's help to please find another way of living. I often hear people say that they always have felt uncomfortable in their skin. Social awkwardness is also mentioned and a desire to "fit in"

At first, I was really blown away by these stories. I felt out of place in my professional work clothes. After a while I decided to start wearing blue jeans and bought a black leather jacket to see if it helped me feel more a part of the group, and it did. Of course not all groups are so diverse. But I am thankful for the diversity of the groups that I attend. It is so refreshing to NOT be judged by my position, looks, or wardrobe. People in Recovery are raw in their honesty. We are each there because all pretenses have been stripped away and we are left with the nakedness of our desperation to find another way to approach life. Perhaps that is why I keep learning from every meeting I attend. The words people say may be the same, but the person saying them is describing a new-found understanding of a concept that is saving their lives. We are all just "becoming." That is so refreshing and humbling at the same time.

I have also come to see the role of the police and judicial system in a new way. I seen how these individuals were the life savers of people in trouble and helped to get them on a new road of life. I've even heard men say that their hope for a way out of life was to be in a confrontation with police and be gunned down. Wow. What a horrible situation for all of those involved. Of course, the people in the meetings are the lucky ones…they have found their way into a solution for their addiction(s). If they are ready to accept it is, of course, dependent on them. I see people come and go. I wonder about the young women who have sat next to me for a while and then one day do not return. Are they o.k? Have they had to go out to "do more experimentation" as it is referred to. I hear it said that we are the lucky ones and I agree with this. We are the "grateful" recovering alcoholics.

There is another aspect of the meeting that I would like to describe.

That is the ethereal aspect of being around and a part of a common openness to God or our Higher Self. The energy of the group of 20 to 30 people holding hands and saying the Lord's Prayer is palpable. I usually leave the meeting feeling "lighter." And so does everyone else, I think. That's why we go. Of course, there are also a few individuals who appear downtrodden and I pray and hope for their relief and comfort.

Have I mentioned the laughter at meetings? It is surprising to find myself laughing as someone describes the silliness of our thoughts and behaviors while we were drinking. We think we are "hiding" it from loved ones who are close to us. Of course, the only person we are really fooling is ourselves. And we keep repeating the same pattern day after day sometimes for years until some event interrupts the pattern and sets us free on the road to Recovery. It may be obvious but perhaps deserves stating that this turning point is seldom anticipated or realized in the moment. Our realization of this diversion into a new way of life is often seen only upon reflection in our sobriety.

My Sponsor

𝒜 sponsor in Recovery is a person, of the same sex, who takes you through the 164 pages of the Big Book [9] and helps you go through the twelve steps.
This is a very intimate journey that is different for each person. I have been most fortunate to have a wonderful sponsor, Amy.

Amy was the secretary of the first Recovery meeting I attended. I was determined to get started in Recovery right away so went up at the end of the meeting and asked her if she would be my sponsor. She graciously accepted. My Higher Power sure knew what it was doing when it put us together. Amy is just the perfect sponsor for me.

From the first day that we met, I have felt comfortable and trusting of Amy and have told her things few people know. She is always attentive, accepting, and loving. She makes suggestions sometimes, but mostly she just listens to what I have to say. Then she might share something from her life that is similar which helps me feel close to her and aware that we are on the right track. We have become good friends and I look forward to our weekly discussions which go way beyond the Big Book reading and into whatever topic is relevant at the moment.

Although Amy is younger than I am, she has the depth of experience and humanity I need to relate to. She is a very caring and warm person.

She is also strong and self-reliant which matches me as well. She is a devoted mother, which I am not, but I honor and appreciate her dedication to her children.

Around Christmas time last year, I came to a meeting directly after watching a movie about losing a loved one. I did not stop to hesitate going even though, as I walked in, I realized I had tears running down by checks. I had watched the movie right around the third anniversary of Leslie's death and the pain from that was ever present at that moment. Although other women in the meeting were warm and supportive, when Amy arrived and took one look at me, she threw her arms around me and asked if I would like to go outside, which I did. We stood outside with her holding me for quite a while and I felt a warmth and love that I so desperately needed to feel. We went back into the meeting and although I cried most of the way through, I felt safe and protected by Amy. It was wonderful.

Amy has many other similarities in terms of family upbringing and values. Our stories are very different but the same in terms of the depths of despair we each felt upon entering the rooms of Recovery. We were both broken and wanting the solution that Recovery has to offer they say in the Big Book, we were "willing to go to any lengths" to stay sober. Our individual willingness opened many doors of insight and connection as we navigated our way into the Recovery lifestyle.

The question of what to look for in a sponsor sometimes comes up in Recovery. From my personal experience I'd say listen to your Higher Power and don't be afraid to ask. You can always choose someone else if that person doesn't turn out to be right. But I think it is important to discuss a change if you are having a problem with your sponsor. The chances are that the problem is with you and the sponsor already knows about it.

Friends

One of the nicest things about going to meetings regularly is that I am surrounded by friends. Each meeting seems to have its own set of people who routinely show up. I look forward to attending a meeting and finding out how everyone is doing. Not that I am particularly outgoing. I am an introvert and quiet by nature. I like to go early and watch as people arrive. I listen to conversations around me and feel comforted by just being there.

The other night I showed up and was feeling unusually tired. One of the men in the group took one look at me and asked me if I was o.k. I explained that I had been going nonstop since early morning and just needed to sit still for a minute. He agreed that I looked tired. The next week he again checked on me. How wonderful to know that he cares.

And that is just the spirit of the room. We all care about each other. I heard it described beautifully a few days ago. It's like we are surrounded by tall, strong pine trees and we aren't allowed to fall too far off center before someone straightens us up again.

It is also fun to run into Recovery members outside of the meeting while I go about my normal routines. We never say where we know each other from, or just say from a support group, to protect anonymity.

I have never felt a part of a group like I do in Recovery except when I was in the Women's Meditation Group with Ardath..

Alzheimer's

Yesterday was particularly difficult. It started out with a text from Eric's mom's caregiver saying they had enjoyed going to the movies Tuesday and had things planned for Saturday so we didn't need to come up, if that was o.k. It was raining, but we went for our walk as usual. As we drove, we discussed what this might mean and how to handle it. Ostensibly it is no big deal. However, it is a change in our schedule and from our experience, his mom will agree to do something in the moment but when the time comes, she is tired and wants to sleep. She has Alzheimer's and what this means for us I do not know. I simply try to take one day at a time and deal with it.

Well we went for our walk, but the park was flooded so we only got in about an hour and a half instead of the usual two hours ok exercise. We decided to call the caregiver after 1:00 when she would be at his mom's. While we were waiting for that, Eric got a phone message from his mom happily saying that they had plans this Saturday so no need to come up. So we called, talked to both of them, and said we thought this a sudden change from our weekly schedule and didn't like the idea. They sounded disappointed.

We took off for our usual Thursday drive up the coast for a treat for us, and we were both upset and trying to figure out what was happening to prompt this change. We called again to get more information and discovered that it was Spring Break so the caregiver's son was home. They had made plans around doing things together at the caregiver's house both weekends including Easter dinner. The caregiver said "I have a new friend and I want to invite here for Easter dinner." That sounds great, however, she is not a friend, she is a client. I feel uncomfortable with her crossing over these boundaries.

I said we needed to discuss it and would call them back. We continued up the coast, driving through some deep puddles in the street, but making it up the highway. He proceeded to get terribly upset because he felt guilty about not letting her go and could not decide what to do. I said that I didn't think his caregiver was realizing that changing the schedule was upsetting for our plans and that asking his mom if she wanted to do something was not the best way to proceed. That she would, of course, say yes in the moment when it sounded fun but the problem with her having Alzheimer's and her general poor state of health, there was no way of telling if she would actually be able to see it through. His mom does not consider what it takes to get something done, how it affects other people, or even how it might impact her. In fact, I would be surprised if she even remembers the conversation the next day. I said that for us, we needed to have a predictable schedule and I wanted to go up Saturday and Sunday as we have a commitment to do and see what happens.

So we called them back. As Eric had feared, his mom was upset with him for saying no to their plans and he felt terrible. So he said to go ahead and asked to talk to the caregiver, which we did. We tried to explain all that we had discussed. It was agreed that they could make plans and try to do them, but we would come up anyway to see how it was going.

The caregiver said she was only trying to make things easier for us, but that did NOT make things easier for us. In fact, it totally upset Eric and I and caused a lot of consternation. We hired her because she said she understood Alzheimer's but now I am beginning to wonder. We shall just have to see what happens on Saturday.

So we were able to have a reasonably relaxing time at dinner and driving home. But on the way home, the road was flooded and as I started to drive across Eric cried out for me to stop and back up. I knew from our previous conversations that I needed to NOT do that and continue driving or else water would get into the muffler and the car would stall. I continued driving and made it across. However, we soon arrived at another road block and he again cried out for me to stop abruptly. Ever since he had the three car accidents at the end of last year he had been hyper-vigilant which is why I drive now, plus I enjoy driving my new car.

We got home and I called my sponsor like I always do at the end of the day. I told her it had been a difficult day but I did not want to relive it by telling her it but would explain when we meet for our usual talk on Saturday mornings.

I came inside and went to bed but could not sleep. I laid awake for two hours because I have so much adrenaline going through my body which I HATE. That is why I exercise so much and do mediation, to regulate that. I did sleep for four hours but am not totally awake. I lie in bed feeling my heart beat. It seems to be stronger than ever before and I can feel it beating hard in my chest. I don't think I have high blood pressure because I take medication for that. But it feels like it is working

hard and I wonder about when it stops one day. Perhaps this is a result of getting regular exercise, the five miles I walk each day. My body is certainly stronger all over more than it ever has been and perhaps my heart is stronger too. I cannot sleep so I decided to get up and write in my journal/book.

I wonder if this can possibly be of interest or use to someone else, to hear about my difficulties and how I try to navigate them. I am still sober although I have certainly had thoughts of having a good strong drink to calm my nerves. But I know I cannot do that so don't.

I do hope this serves some useful purpose other than just getting it all off of my mind. Oh well, that's now I feel now. I'm going to go lie down now and try to at least let my body rest even if my mind isn't. I'll do some meditation and praying also. Perhaps that will help.

Uncertainty

I want to try to write about something that is not clearly in my head yet. But maybe if I try to describe it the words will come. It has to do with the experience I now live with of total uncertainty. Perhaps life has always been uncertain, but I never felt that way before. Today is a hard day.

Today I doubt myself and my life.

Something about Leslie dying and then the water heater going out in our home and causing huge damage to the house that took six months to repair has caused me to realize that I live with uncertainty every day. It's like I used to think that I understood life, what was required to live it "successfully". I had certain standards that I tried to live up to and was generally able to do so. Now I am painfully aware that I don't know what to do or how to do it. It's as though I had a compass and lost it. I thought there were standards and principles to live up to and if done correctly life would reward me with ease and comfort. Instead I now have financial independence and total freedom to do as I please and I feel adrift. There are many hours each day which need to be filled in as meaningful a way as I can manage. It helps to start with the walk. That takes three hours by the time I drive up and back to the lake. Then we have a bite to eat out at our favorite local restaurant where many locals go. I have activities structured for each day and for the week, but it feels like I am trying to get by doing what seems like a meaningful life but isn't. I want to structure my time so that it is wisely spent so include an hour watching the PBS Newshour each day if possible. I attend a Recovery meeting which definitely feels meaningful to me and to others in attendance and is a wonderful way to wrap up the day. I am writing this book which seems purposeful but I wonder if it really is.

It's not like anyone else in the world has it better figured out than me.

I think I am just aware of the existential pain of feeling that my life is somehow over, that the productive days of certainty of purpose are over. I knew how much I needed to work in order to pay my bills and did so willingly. Now all absolutes have vanished.

I do believe that we are each here on earth in our respective lives to learn lessons unique to each of us. And when we have learned them I believe we die. So, it is something like a graduation, a celebration that hard work has been accomplished and we've earned the right to go back home to God. But in the meantime, I am treading water as best I can, going through the motions of having a meaningful life, without really knowing that I am, that I am doing it "right" whatever that is.

It is hard for me to live like this. I try not to think about it. But I feel very ready to let go of this life and move on. In fact, I long for it, to be done. I do appreciate the beauty of life but it's not enough for me anymore. I am going through the motions. I don't plan to kill myself because I honestly don't think that would solve the problem: if I have not finished doing what I came here to do I would simply have to be reborn and do it all over again, which I don't want to do. I find myself watching people and wondering if I came back as them if I would want to do so; if the joy of their life would make it worth all of the suffering that comes along with it. I think about it and always come up with the answer that, no, that would not entice me to return. I may sound ungrateful for the blessings of my life. I am grateful but there is still something missing. Today I miss feeling beautiful and young and full of promise. Today I miss having goals for myself and accomplishing them, such as, getting a Black Belt or a PhD or becoming an Associate Vice President. I did all of these things. And I left and moved on because a part of my soul was longing for more. A part of me was suffering in those roles and I felt isolated from myself, living just a part of me out in each situation. Now I feel authentic all of the time. I do not hide. I am honest. I usually elect to share very little of myself with others. It usually seems unnecessary to talk. I wonder at how people can talk endlessly about nothing. It's almost as if some people are talking about their lives and asking me "does this matter?" "Are you impressed with this fact about me?" I feel a pressure from them to respond and reaffirm their lives but I do not respond. I think about if there is something I can honestly say that would contribute to the discussion, but I generally cannot think of anything, partly because I think they are talking about nothing. They are simply rambling on about their lives.

What I do find meaningful is Recovery meetings. Here we discuss the thorny topics of life: What does surrender mean? What do I do about the boredom in my life? How do I handle depression? What is gratitude, service, or Recovery? In Recovery there is no room for pretense. Everyone who stays is authentic. I see people leave and I usually feel from them a level of pretense. I don't mean this in a condemning way. I mean it to be that they are still holding onto an image of themselves as being o.k. and are not ready to fully surrender to the process discussed in meetings and in the Big Book. A level of desperation is required to be willing to give up all that has taken us through life until the point of walking through those doors and be willing to try something new. It is humbling yet liberating. Fortunately at that point we can rely on others in the group to care for us and love us in a way we have not yet known. Usually shame and defeat are the feelings utmost in our minds when we fearfully walk through the doors. We have been beaten by life. And then slowly we begin the journey back to life. We do what is suggested to us to do. Or we can choose to leave and try once again to get by on our old coping strategies.

Maybe today I feel so uncertain because I am "becoming" rather than "being" I said to my sponsor that I feel like I step out into each day like off of a cliff onto air trusting that I will not fall. I say my prayers first thing each morning on the faith and hope that there really IS a Higher Power here to help me. I say that even though I have had many times in my life when that Higher Power has proven Itself to be guiding me and helping me. What part of me keeps holding back in fear? What part of me is still in pain? I am not sure. This is what I am pondering. Tomorrow may be different.

My Private Safe Place

Frances asked me if I could talk more about the dark, safe place that I retreat to sometimes. I had mentioned it in therapy last week. It is a place inside myself that is still, quiet and safe.

I believe I developed this place inside me when I was a child. I felt that I had to live up to standards of perfection when I was a child. I had to dress just right, excel in school, and act in a prescribed way in every situation. It's like life had already been figured out by my parents and they gave me their blueprint for success. I just had to obey and behave as they wanted me to.

But there were always times when I wanted to retreat and be alone. I remember as a child when we lived on the lake that I would wonder in the woods by myself and be quite and at peace. I loved to watch and hear the birds. I remember one day I took the row boat out and was watching some fish in the water next to the boat. I picked one up and looked at it. It was beautiful. Then I gently laid it back into the water and it swam away.

I used to enjoy rowing by myself, feeling safe to explore and be with nature. One day I rowed up to the top of the canal where a bridge crossed over the water. I saw a burlap bag handing down into the water and feared that someone has drowned some kittens in the water. I came home and got my sister. We rowed up together and tentatively untied the bag and looked inside. It had clorine in it to kill the algae in the lake. What a relief that was for us

I remember walking home from school through the woods enjoying the beauty and peacefulness of it all. One day in fall I walked home and I got my clothes dirty and got in trouble for that. I was more careful from them on.

What I'm trying to say is that I've always had a special private place inside me where I can be alone and safe, away from the demands of family and other people. So for me, to retreat is to find solace. It is much preferable to the noise and business of being around other people.

Today I withdraw there when I feel tired and overwhelmed. I enjoy being apart. I enjoy the quiet and peace. It is not a depression or sad space. It is the part of me that does not change, is not connected to the striving and performance of the many tasks I have set up for myself or society has set up for me to attend to. Non-striving is what I am talking about. Just being.

My Heart

It has been an unusual day. I woke up at 2:00 a.m. and could not go back to sleep. Finally, I started meditating asking God if there was anything I needed to pay attention to. My heart was beating very hard, as I've noticed lately. I was feeling my body breathe in each breath and my heart beating along with the rhythm and thought to myself I am only one breath away from being dead. I wonder when it will stop. That led me to think about how upset Eric would be if I were to die suddenly and he wouldn't know what to do. So in my head I thought of all of the things he should know from calling the mortuary to pick up my body (which I have prepaid to be cremated) to handling the bills and how to do a memorial if he would like. I didn't get up to write in my journal because I thought maybe I could get a little more sleep. I finally did dose off around 6:30 for an hour.

I awoke at 9:00 a.m. the time I get up every morning to go for our walk. It was still raining hard so I thought I'd write on my computer the things I wanted Eric to know if I passed so I could get that off of my mind. When I finished I went downstairs to see Eric. as much as I wanted to go for a walk, it was pouring down rain so we decided to go out for breakfast. During breakfast I told him about what I had been up to. I also noticed that he was talking a lot about the past when he was a surfer and how he used to do things. I asked him to focus instead on the moment and what we might do together in the future. He got my point. One thing we want to do is go horseback riding on the coast so we will stop at one of the ranches we pass each week and figure out when we can do that.

It was still raining after breakfast so we decided to go to the movies.

We walked in and a movie was just starting that sounded good: The

Miracle Season. It was a wonderful movie about a true story of a high school volleyball player names Caroline Found who passed suddenly and how her team rallied and won the State Championship in Iowa 2011 in her honor. It was very moving.

Surrender

Surrender is that moment when we realize and acknowledge to our innermost selves that we cannot stop drinking, that the option to "not drink" has been removed, that will power and desire to stop drinking have no effect to change our behavior. We may use different internal and external words like "I need help" or "I cannot do this anymore" or "I'm through living in this hell." Before surrender, our life is one of attempts to manage and control our drinking and everything else in our life. These efforts are futile. But it may take us many years to realize the reality of that statement. Negative consequences are usually rationalized away or ignored so that we can shift our attention to our "go to," to alcohol. Alcohol seems to be the answer to every situation in our lives: anxiety, sadness, relief, joy, celebration, feeling down… The mental preoccupation with alcohol can only be understood by an alcoholic. In the back of one's mind is always the thought "do I have enough alcohol on hand for today" or "when can I take my next drink" or "I need more." Life seems to be lived in a hurry to get to the reward, to "get to the next drink." I'm sure you know what I'm talking about.

Surrender is our moment of release from the powerful hold alcohol has on us. It is a moment of sanity and humility: we realize we do not have the answer to our lives, that our best efforts have left us broken, ashamed, humiliated, and defeated. Yet it is exactly in this moment that we are released and begin to feel the freedom from alcohol. We begin to learn how to live a completely new life. We "let go" and "let God."

Gradually surrender becomes a daily practice. Many of us start the day with the Third Step Prayer, *I offer myself to Thee, to build with me and to do with me as Thou wilt...* We learn to *pause when agitated;* to stop our automatic response to a situation, relax, and find our *soul's integrity.* We look for opportunities to serve others. Our life has a new meaning. This is the gift of sobriety.

Gratitude

Gratitude for me is a matter of perception. It usually requires that I shift the kaleidoscope of my perception a few degrees away from my normal gaze and onto one of more light, beauty, and love. Often this shift is thrust upon me like when I am driving North up Highway 1 and I turn a curve in the road revealing a breathtaking view of the expanse of the Pacific Ocean with rocks and waves below the cliffs. Or when I suddenly glance up and see the blue sky above with soft white clouds drifting by.

> I find myself grateful for nature
> A soft yellow duckling in the Spring
> Hearing the wind blowing through the trees
> A bee landing upon a flower
> The hooting of a barn owl in my backyard at night.
> I find myself grateful for people in my life
> Friends who greet me at Recovery meeting
> The safety and comfort I feel snuggled in bed next to my beloved
> Looking into the loving eyes of my sponsor
> Meeting a new sponsee and seeing the wonder and hope in their eyes.
> I am grateful for physical health
> For being able to walk five miles every day
> For waking up sober and turning my life over to a Higher
> For being able to see, hear, smell, and touch
> For feeling the strength in my legs.

But most of all I am grateful for the gift of sobriety for without it I would not be experiencing any of the things listed above. I would be lost in a prison of my own making yet not knowing any way out. I remember my last drunk and am humbled to my knees at the incredible transformation that has occurred in my life since walking into the rooms of Recovery. A new way of living full of grace and opportunity has emerged out of the darkness. All that was required was surrender and trust.

Living in the Presence

In Recovery we learn to live in what is referred to as *the fourth dimension*. This is a powerful shift in consciousness. When I came into Recovery I was full of fear. The past was over, the present included profound grief over the loss of my wife of 20 years, and the future was bleak. I was lost in fear and had sought solace in alcohol. That lead me to deeper despair and suicidal attempts. I was confused and did not understand what was happening to me.

From the first moment I walked into the rooms of Recovery I knew I was powerless over alcohol and that my life had become unmanageable. Being raised Lutheran it was easy for me to believe in a Power greater than myself including all of my new friends as well as a Creative Loving Energy I had turned away from years earlier. I trusted the group and the process.

With each meeting, each exchange with another person in Recovery, every new day in sobriety, I learned to let go of the past, quit anticipating the future, and experience the NOW, the present moment. And the more I did that, prayed and meditated, I became aware of the PRESENCE which is an experience of the Diving unfolding in every person and situation. A new-found peace began to emerge and lasted longer and longer each day.

Today I practice the PRESENCE , that is, I constantly try to have my focus be on the wholeness and beauty of each moment. I remind myself, when I get anxious, that I have everything I need AT THIS MOMENT. Nothing more is required for me to feel peace and serenity…just to let go and BE IN THE MOMENT. This is much more than relief from alcohol, it is a profound new way of living that I am learning and practicing in each moment. How blessed I am!

Doubt

There are times when I lose my grip on life. Some unexpected news shatters my normal equanimity: a sudden need for surgery for a loved one, financial set back, someone close to me is dishonest... I find myself caught up in fear. I struggle to make sense of it all. I lose my perspective that things are unfolding as they should according to a plan beyond my comprehension. I lose my faith.

At these times I reach out to familiar coping mechanisms. I go to a meeting. I call my sponsor. I pray and meditate. I go back to basics: I am an alcoholic, my life is unmanageable at this moment, I need to turn my will and my life over to a power greater than myself.

Still I may stay in these uncomfortable feelings for days. I long for each day to be over as each minute seems like a struggle to find serenity and I just want to close my eyes and wake up to a new day. I put one step in front of the other and do not pick up a drink because I remember my last bottom and do not want to go through that again. Alcohol is not an answer for a reprieve.

The past few days have been like that. I'm in a learning phase. Today I went for a two hour walk with my sponsor. Walking around Spring Lake in the rain was wonderful. There were few people there and we could talk and share. She reminded me of the basics, we worked through a current resentment which was causing my mental upheaval. But beyond the techniques and suggestions, I felt her love. She didn't have to have all the answers for me, I just needed to feel that I was not alone, that someone cared, that I fit into the pattern of life. I needed to pause and feel the comfort of grace that is always available but that I had forgotten. The peace of the walk, the loving guidance, and the grace of the moment healed my fears and reminded me that I am a part of the unfolding mystery around me. We are each an essential part of the whole. That is why we are here. We matter.

Being of Service

Being of Service is a way of life in Recovery. It is suggested, soon upon entering the rooms of Recovery, that we take on a service commitment, usually making coffee. This is a wonderful way to get to know other people in Recovery. You need to arrive early, take out the necessary equipment, put on the coffee, and wait for others to arrive. It feels a little awkward at first, not knowing anyone, but gradually you get to know people as they arrive and come over to help themselves to coffee and chat with you in a friendly sort of way. It feels good to be contributing to others, to be of service

When I first started attending Recovery meetings I went to six meetings a week and had three service commitments. I tried coffee, literature, and gradually took on "secretary" or the person who runs the meetings. I felt honored that others wanted me to contribute in these ways. I got used to being in front of the crown talking. I even got a little rowdy toward the end of my secretary commitment ready to try new things, to shake things up a little. Soon I found myself knowing just about everybody's name. I was a part of Recovery.

That service has continued to grow. And I now realize that I had begun to shift my focus away from selfish things and onto my fellows. We can only focus on one thing at a time. If we are paying attention to others, we are not paying attention to ourselves. Our world expands to include others.

Perhaps the most wonderful thing we can experience is taking another through the Recovery process, through the steps, is seeing the light come on in their eyes. Love and service, that is what Recovery means to me. And with that comes freedom from myself and a life of purpose beyond what I could ever have imagined. One step at a time, one day at a time, my life has grown to include many new friends and loved ones. I feel an integral part of bringing Recovery to the world. What better activity is there?

Intellectual Influences on the Twelve Steps

It is well known that the *Twelve Steps of Alcoholics Anonymous* [1] were developed by Bill W (William Griffith Wilson), [13] Doctor Bob (Bob Smith,) [14] and 100 members of that fledgling society in the 1930's in the United States. [9] At that time and still today, members adhered to a strict code of anonymity so as to not jeopardize their standing in the community, get an inflated sense of self, or be overwhelmed by requests for help. Since that day, The *Twelve Steps*, as they are affectionately known in recovery circles, have been recognized as an important intellectual contribution and spiritual tool not only in the treatment of alcoholism but many other problems such as drug abuse, gambling abuse, sexual abuse, over eating and the many various ineffective ways that individuals use to cope with stresses in their lives. They were first published in the book *Alcoholics Anonymous* in 1939. [9] Contemporaries of Bill W. included William James, Carl Gustaf Jung, and a Lutheran Minister named Frank Buckman.

The Twelve Steps are listed below.

1. We admitted we were powerless over alcohol – that our lives had become unmanageable.
2. Came to believe that a Power greater than ourselves could restore us to sanity.
3. Made a decision to turn our will and our lives over to the care of God <u>as we understood Him</u>.

4. Made a searching and fearless moral inventory of ourselves.
5. Admitted to God, to ourselves, and to another human being the exact nature of our wrong.
6. Were entirely ready to have God remove all these defects of character.
7. Humbly ask Him to remove our shortcomings.
8. Made a list of all persons we had harmed, and because willing to make amends to them all.
9. Made direct amends to such people whenever possible, except when to do so would injure them or others.
10. Continued to take personal inventory and when we were wrong promptly admitted it.
11. Sought through prayer and meditation to improve our conscious contact with God <u>as we understood Him</u>, praying only for knowledge of His will for us and the power to carry that out.
12. Having had a spiritual awakening as a result of these steps, we tried to carry this message to alcoholics, and to practice these principles in all our affairs.

The first major influence on the development of The Twelve Steps was the Oxford Group, founded by the Lutheran Minister Frank Buckman, of which Dr. Bob was a member. [4] Bill W. visited the group also.

"Members of the Oxford Group sought to achieve spiritual regeneration by making a surrender to God through rigorous self-examination, confessing their character defects to another human being, making restitution for harm done to others, and giving without thought of reward – or, as they put it: 'No pay for soul surgery.' They did, however, accept contributions." [4]

They advocated listening to God's guidance, and carrying it out.

The Oxford Group developed six steps to accomplish this goal. [8]
1. A Complete deflation.
2. Dependence on God.
3. A Moral inventory.
4. Confession.
5. Restitution.

The Six Steps, developed by the Oxford Group [6], look surprisingly like the steps in the Twelve Steps, specifically:

Number	Oxford Group Steps	Twelve Steps of Alcoholics Anonymous Number
1	A Complete deflation	1
2	Dependence on God	2, 3, 6, 7, 11
3	A Moral inventory.	4
4	Confessions	5
5	Restitution.	8, 9, 10
6	Continues work with others in need.	12

It is clear that the Twelve Steps operationalize and further expand on the Oxford Steps. For example, *Dependence on God* is dealt with in five steps in the Twelve Step Program (2, 3, 6, 7, 11) and *Restitution* is dealt with in three steps (8, 9, 10). This change was based upon their extensive experience in working with alcoholics and trying to help them understand and apply the concepts.

It should be noted that the Twelve Step Program is basically a spiritual one, based on love and service. The Third Step is the essential step of giving one's life to a Higher Power. The Third Step pray reads (Big Book, page 83) [9]:

God I offer myself to Thee, to build with me and to do with me as Thou Wilt. Relieve me of the bondage of self so that I may better do Thy Will. Take away my difficulties so victory over them may bear witness to those I would help of Thy Love, Thy Power, and Thy Way of Life. May I do Thy Will always.

This level of surrender to God or a High Power is equivalent to William James' discussion of Conversion in *The Varieties of Religious Experience Lecture IX. Conversion and Lecture X. Conversion – Concluded* [2]. James describes conversion as

"To be converted, to be regenerated, to receive grace, to experience religion, to gain an assurance, as so many phrases which denote the process, gradual or sudden, by which a self hitherto divided, and consciously wrong inferior and unhappy, becomes unified and consciously right superior and happy. (p. 5).

James relates accounts of personal conversion in these essays. Phrases used to describe this transition in consciousness include "the power of the Holy Spirit" (p. 57), "feel[ing] exceedingly happy and humble" (p. 57), and "utterly full of the love and grace of God" (p. 58). "We tend to speak of the phenomenon, and perhaps to wonder at it, as a 'transformation'" (p. 58). A description of this experience is expressed in Twelve Step recovery meetings, although it is rare, with most people reporting a gradual reliance on a Higher Power. The degree of surrender depends on the level of need of the individual, with very desperate individuals being ready and willing for a complete surrender necessary for this transformation.

Bill W. was also corresponding with Carl Gustaf Jung about his ideas from 1945 until his death in 1961.[15] In a letter written January 30, 1941, Jung comments on a previous patient, Roland H., who had subsequently gone to AA for help. Jung confirmed that the way out of the level of despair and disintegration that Roland H. presented was through a complete spiritual experience, a complete reliance on the Divine or "Higher Power." Jung states that Roland's "craving for alcohol was the quivalent on a low level of the spiritual thirst for wholeness, expressed in midieval language, union with God."

Alcohol, which is often referred to as "spirits," is a false God, an inadequate way of meeting the real spiritual thirst of not only an alcoholic, but any outer obsession used to cope and hopefully get spiritual satisfaction. This is very prevalent in our society, and around the world today. We can all benefit from a refocus on methods and practices which actually meet these needs such as community, spiritual readings and services, chanting (Gregorian and Sanscrit), music, nature (sunsets, sunrises, the magnificence of the ocean and mountains…), meditation, prayer (listening to our inner guidance) and paying attention to the synchronicity of life, guidance found in dreams and insights, creative expression and the various ways that we connect to the Eternal Essence underlying all things or what Jung calls in Latin, the *Unus Mundus*.

The Twelve Steps is a well-articulated path for such a transition. It is similar to other spiritual practices and ideas. For example "rigorous honesty" is "right speech" in Buddhism, "One day at a time" is "staying in the present" (Buddhism), "the forth an fifth steps inventories and sharing" are equivalent to "confessions of sins" in the Catholic religion and "missing the mark" in Judaism, "making amends" equals "do unto others and forgiveness" of Christianity, and "turning your will over to God" is "Trust in God" in Christianity. [16] The spiritual principles of Science of Mind, founded by Ernest Holmes around the same time as AA, are quite similar to the Twelve Steps of AA, although Homes got his guidance and intellectual foundations from books by Ralph Waldo Emerson (a Transcendentalist along with Henry David Thoreau and others), Thomas Troward, and Emma Curtis Hopkins. These concepts include One Divine Principle (God in AA), the benefits of connection to the Divine through meditation and prayer, and Positive Mind Treatment, similar to William James' concept of Healthy-Mindedness which we will deal with in the next section. There are many paths to the same destination. They are all of value.

PART TWO

The Center for Spiritual Living

This Part of my story reflects some of my thoughts from Recovery and from the past eighteen months studying and attending The Center for Spiritual Living in Santa Rosa, California. This Center is based on the teaching of Ernest Holmes called Science of Mind. In December 2018 I was year and a half into sobriety and feeling a deep spiritual pull to go deeper in my connection with the Divine. Recovery had opened my heart to a Higher Power and my life was transforming according to God's will, not mine. I was experiencing moments of awareness of the Divine in my life, unfolding in the moment with everyone and everything that I saw around me. I was talking to a friend in Recovery and he suggested that I try the Center for Spiritual Living located in our city. I thought about it but did not act upon it. Then another person in Recovery said the same thing to me, but I ignored it again (obviously not following the Divine Guidance I was receiving). Finally, in early January I was having breakfast alone at my favorite local coffee shop reading *The Sermon and the Mount* by Emmet Fox when the man at the table next to me asked if I was enjoying my book. I said I was and he said "if you like that, you might try the Center for Spiritual Living." I finally heard the guidance and decided to go that next week.

I looked up the Center on the web and saw that there was a free discussion on the principles of the Center on Wednesday evenings. I went to that meeting. It was an introduction to the Science of Mind as taught by

Ernest Holmes which serves as the basis for their teachings and work. There I felt the Divine all around me and wanted to know how to handle that energy. Was I in the right place?" They assured me that I was and I felt reassured.

Sunday, I went to the regular service and was inspired the service and a sermon by Reverend Edward Viljoen. I went again the next Wednesday and learned that they were starting classes on understanding the teaching of the Center. I signed up for one to begin the next week: a ten-week class on the Basic Concepts of Science of Mind. I was excited and felt I was on the right track.

Old Thought vs. New Thought

I am in my first class called *Basic Principles of the Science of Mind*. I am excited to be embarking on a new field of study. The first class was spent discussing the difference between Old Thought and New Thought in terms of a religions understanding. Old theology taught ideas of good and evil, it was fear based, Divinity was perceived of as being outside ourselves, arbitrary, and there were strict rules regarding our thoughts and behaviors. New Though is characterized by the concept of one power that is love-based, the idea that we are evolving to a higher Good, we are one with Divinity, our thoughts are creative and we are perfect and whole. We then spent time listing all of the names of God that we could recall.

There are two phases of mind: surface mind which is our consciousness and deep mind which is our unconscious or subconscious mind. Our thoughts are creative. They move from consciousness to deeper mind which then prompts the manifestations of our life. The central idea is that the Universe says "yes" to our thoughts. Therefore, our life represents our thoughts, conscious and unconscious. It is analogous to a loom on which a weaver weaves cloth. The Universe is the loom and our thoughts are creating the cloth of our experiences. Hence it is very important to explore and bring to consciousness thoughts which we absorbed from our family and society which govern our lives, even though we don't know it. The creation of our life through conscious and unconscious thoughts is called the Law of Cause and Effect. The task in life is to become more conscious of our thoughts which are habitual and constant. A change in our thoughts will lead to a change in life circumstances.

Material thinking is focused on what is outside of us. Spiritual thinking is focused on what is happening inside us; our connection to God. In Science of Mind, we turn away from external circumstances and focus on the internal mind state that we wish to manifest in our lives. We learn to do Spiritual Mind Treatment, which is a method of shifting our focus from the causes of suffering in our life to the qualities of God that replace this error in consciousness. Qualities of God, the Divine Essence, include peace, serenity, loving kindness, harmony, power, beauty, wisdom, and so forth.

The first step in building a consciousness of our true worth is letting go of negative thinking. We do not get caught in self-blame for our problems and suffering in our past, we see the past as a learning process. We shift our focus to positive statements. This is more than positive thinking and affirmations. It is a radical shift in consciousness from error to Truth. Power flows from the focus of our attention. So, we start with moving our attention to positive, uplifting statements about ourselves and others. We then attract to us what we have focused on which is the Law of Attraction. We let go of negative attitudes because hostility, judgments, and resentments toward others bock the flow of Divine creativity. The attitude we must take toward those who have hurt us is forgiveness.

The practical application of these principles can be experienced by (1) listing the desired conditions for your life and (2) listing the qualities that the River of Perfect Mind will manifest in your life. For example: I have a desired condition of sobriety, love shared between me and my husband, physical health and daily exercise, meaningful work, and prosperity. The qualities I want manifested in my life are love, joy, peace, abundance, and physical healing. The affirmations need to be in the present tense ("I am…") and affirmative ("I am…" vs "I am not…". They need to be believable to you at this time.

I was participating fully in the class activities. However, a part of me was holding back thinking: this is someone else's conclusions about how the Universe works. I'm not sure it is mine. What I was aware of was that I could sense Divine energy in me and others and in between us. I also sensed that most people were blocking this energy. I wanted to learn how to direct the energy in a positive way for myself and other people. I did feel that this teaching might help me learn how to do that.

Spirit, Mind, Body

One of the central concepts that we were taught was that God is composed of Spirit, Mind and Body. We similarly are composed of spirit, mind, and body. This was taught by drawing two circles. In the one on the left, the three aspects of God were listed. On the right were the concepts of humans presented. We were asked to draw this in our notebooks while the instructor Reverend Joyce Duffala walked around to check on our progress. Well when I was thinking about this during our reading before class, it seemed to me that rather than having two circles, I ought to draw one circle with a perpendicular line down the middle dividing into two equal parts on each side. Then each side had two parallel lines separating the Spirit (spirit), Mind (mind), and Body (body). I thought it was obvious: if God was everything why would there be a separate circle? When Joyce saw my figure she said "this is brilliant". I was flattered and encouraged.

Healing

The Body of God is the Universe. The body of humans is our life, body, all that which is manifest in our lives. The great significance in healing is the fact that our physical body is characterized by inertia: it stays going in the direction it is headed. If it is still, it stays still. If it is moving in a certain direction, it stays moving in that direction. The creator of the body is our thoughts. In Science of Mind, we say there are no incurable diseases because there is no limit to our acceptance of the truth of our wholeness. When results are not forthcoming when we think they should be, we should constantly shift of our awareness to the thoughts of what we want to create in our lives. Healing is a shift in consciousness. There is in fact nothings to heal. We are naturally whole, healthy and complete. However, we have forgotten that.

What I am getting from our instructor Joyce is a sense of validation for who I am. I am also receiving the gift of paying attention to others and what their needs and wants are.

We did an exercise today at the start of class that was very upsetting to me. The meditation was to remember being with someone or in a situation where we felt loved. I immediately thought of Leslie, my wife of twenty years who passed away four years ago, and tears began to roll down my face. I could not stop crying. Every time I tried to focus on what we were being taught, I was overwhelmed with grief. I finally asked one of the Practitioners in the class to help me. I went out with Tom. I told him what I was feeling and he comforted me saying "of course you are feeling this way. You ARE love and your love for Leslie is what you are experiencing." I felt a huge sigh of relief and relaxation. I just let that reality sink into my being. I was overcome again with emotion and this time it was joy, the joy of KNOWING I AM LOVE. The grief, where I was pushing away my love of Leslie because it hurt so much for her to be gone, was replaced by my moving INTO that love and finding relief. That feeling stayed with me for a long time.

Spiritual Mind Treatment

We are now studying Spiritual Mind Treatment, or a type of affirmative prayer that is used for healing. The foundation of authority is *knowing*. What bearing does this have on healing the physical body? When we know it is already done (the healing), it is accomplished. We are exploring the Law of Creation. We can manifest *anything* in Spirit/Mind. In Science of Mind, we are encouraged to apply the principles we are learning to our own lives until we *experience* the reality of them. Then we know that they work. It is not an intellectual exercise. It is a matter of belief and then experience.

"And suddenly you know, it's time to start something new and trust the magic of new beginnings." Meister Eckhart

There are five steps in a Spiritual Mind Treatment. In Spiritual Mind Treatment we are changing the consciousness of the Practitioner about the perceived condition in the Client. We align our consciousness to the Truth in which the condition does not exist. It is done in the NOW. And when it is done, it is finished and complete. We start by getting into a relaxed state of mind. The steps are:

Recognition of the truth of Spirit: that it is unconditional love, omnipresent, omnipotent, and omniscient.

Unification: that we are an individualized expression of the Divine, a part of Spirit, and so is the person we are treating for.

Realization: We realize that the condition is false and align with the truth of our being. We see the quality of the Divine that replaces the condition we see in our Client's life. God is light, life, joy, beauty, love, peace and power.

Thanksgiving: We give thanks for the reality of this truth.

Release: We acknowledge that it has already been changed in consciousness and will continue to unfold in our affairs as time moves forward.

I am now practicing using Spiritual Mind Treatment to deal with people and situations that are disturbing me. I find when I go through the steps, my mind is re-centered in the truth of life and shifted away from the disturbance of the lack that I am perceiving. I am finding more peace and serenity. I am finding a way to heal my consciousness.

Projections

Just came home from my class on the philosophical roots of Ernest Holmes and Science of Mind. We were discussing how our innermost assumptions about life keep being manifested in our lives until we can see and confront them once again. I said "well it sounds like we are just projecting onto the world." The instructor Rev. Ruth Barnhart said "Yes." "Then the logical consequence of that is that we will continue to remove our projections until we are finally faced with Truth which is Love. Then we will probably want to return and help others remove their projections," I said. "Yes, that is what all of the Master's have done" she replied.

Wow! I think I finally get it!

Another quote we discussed from Emerson is "Our faith comes in moments; our vice is habitual." (Emerson's Essays, p. 188) (18). What this means to me is that we need to be constantly working on changing our assumptions about the world to see Truth and start recreating the reality that reflects these assumptions. Again, I see my life repeating patterns of relationships that reflect how I assume they should work. Right now, I am aware of a pattern of codependent reactions with Eric and we are now in counseling for me to try to understand my part in this and, of course, for him to understand his part in it. It's quite exciting. I don't feel a sense of blame but rather a sense of excitement about recognizing these patterns and changing them.

As they say in Recovery and in Science of Mind: "How free do you want to be?"

I realize that I want to return to reading A Course in Miracles (19) for in it Jesus talks about how we are projecting our perceptions onto the world.

I went for my walk to day and realized I am feeling uplifted by Spirit just like the birds I saw who were gracefully floating on the wind currents. I simply have to let go and let God.

Seed Thought

In class week, we were asked to conceive of a "seed thought" that we would like to see materialized by the end of the class or longer. What immediately came to mind for me was this book and its unfolding. We were to state what the "seed thought" was and then notice each day as evidence of Divine Guidance came to us from our lives.

I am amazed at how smoothly and consistently this book unfolding is happening. It is just like with my first book. It is almost writing itself. And each day I get a prompt from an email to go one step further with the process. This morning it was an email from the CEO of the film production company that is interested in possible doing a short documentary. He included specific instructions of what I need to do to qualify. I have most criteria but have a few to go including a screen play of my first book, a "Hollywood treatment", and "pitch materials." Fortunately, I was contacted by someone a few months ago offering to do just that. I told that person I would get back to them after the Canada book signing events. I sent that person an email saying I would like to proceed.

It is just like the first book; each day a little something happens that prompts me to believe that it is God's will for these materials to be released to the public. I know there is a great need in our culture for a contemporary female voice in Recovery. I have certainly contributed in my own small way in shifting the trend of seeing women as subservient to men to people of their own right with the ability to work professionally, handling both family and job at the same time.

I am sure it is hard for women of today to even comprehend such archaic thinking as women not being able to have a career and home. But I lived through the 1950's where that was certainly the case. Women stayed home, took care of the children and their husband, and were subservient in every way. Thank God that has changed some.

Women's Retreat

I'm at my first Annual Recovery Women's Retreat in the redwoods in Northern California. I've never been around so many women at one time, around 150. I'm used to conferences that used to be dominated by men and I watch as women gradually were added to become equal in number to the men. This has a completely different feel. I am a little uncomfortable.

This is yoga time 7:00 – 8:00 a.m. But I am spoiled when it comes to studying yoga in the United States because I was instructed by a teacher from India, Pondurangadas. He used to be a Long Shoreman in New York. In the 1960's he left that job, moved to India, and came back a thin spiritual and yoga teacher.

I don't remember how I met him. He was living in Berkeley at the time in the 1970's. I invited him to come teach an all-day yoga workshop at the small town where I was going to college. He can and it was wonderful!

He taught that yoga is about "yoking" or "connecting to God." Pondurangadas taught that Yatha Yoga was about paying attention to the body; finding that point in your body in a pose where you have stretched as far as you can then exhaling into it which causes a natural relaxing of the body and stretching a little bit further. It was NOT about "getting into a stance"; it was about noticing the point of resistance and softening into it. I also think, now, that that was an analogy to paying attention to each moment's consciousness.

I've studied Hatha Yoga in the United States and have found it most disappointing. The instructors invariably focus on reaching a certain position. It has been Westernized into an external focus of achievement – so typical of our society. This misses the essential point.

One summer day in the 1970'2 I felt drawn to go to an outdoor festival at a city near where I was going to college. I was walking around by myself and I spotted Pondurangadas in the crowd. We walked toward each other and embraced. He pulled back and said "so you are why I am here. I was wondering why I was coming today." We strolled around together and he found for me a used copy of the Bhagavad Gita which I purchased and read.

Guided Meditation in the Redwood Glen

I just went for a group guided meditation in a grove of very old and majestic redwood trees. As I laid down to rest and hear the meditation, when I looked up, I was awestruck by the beauty above. The tops of the grove of trees made a canopy that was filled with light.

What caught my attention was a very tall redwood gently swaying in the wind. It gracefully rocked back and forth with the top one third of its majestic 750 feet trunk rocking repeatedly back and forth. When the meditation music started to play, I started to cry at the beauty of the moment. I borrowed a friend's cell phone to capture a picture of it at that perfect moment.

The meditation went on for a half hour but I was fixed on the pageantry above. I heard redwood needles drop occasionally and one pine cone fall. I was mesmerized.

A Spirit Walk

Tonight, we did a "spirit walk." It consisted of two lines of women facing each other and then each one of us took turns being blind folded and led down that line. Each woman in the line walked up to the woman in the middle, touched her shoulder, and spoke into their ear some positive statement about her.

The affirmation that hit my core was "Rose, you **are** good enough" or "Rose you are worthy." This hit my deep wound from childhood thinking I was "not good enough." I was never told this directly, rather the opposite. I was told I could do anything I set my mind to. But the feeling of "not good enough" somehow passed into my unconscious. It came from society at the time and probably from my family as well and generations before that. This is the message that has spurred me on my whole life to achieve difficult things like my Black Belt in Ju Jitsu and two doctorates. I figured a doctorate from the University of California Berkeley would finally allow me to speak my mind and be taken seriously. It certainly helped. But nothing could erase that subtle voice of doubt and uncertainty, that voice of unworthiness. I needed to learn to listen to and trust my inner wisdom, my intuition, which is what I am doing now.

I have tried hard to change this belief of unworthiness. It is finally melting away thanks all of the love and unconditional love I am receiving in Recovery and from my spiritual unfolding. I have learned to trust my inner wisdom, my intuition. This is a feeling of "knowing" my truth, experiencing my truth and my connection with my Higher Power. I am now recognizing myself to be an Individualized Expression of the Divine, a unique manifestation of the Great Spirit. What a healing. What a blessing!

Four Swans Flying

On my walk this morning I was suddenly startled by the loud sound of four swans flying by me across the lake. They were very close and I could hear their wings going *swish swish* in the air loud and clear. It was breathtaking.

Recently I have come to the awareness that I am becoming a metaphysician. This is particularly touching to me as my early adult goal was to become a physician. As I have grown and experienced more in life, I have realized my interest is not so much in the body but in the mind and spirit. Being a Jungian Therapist was a goal in my 30's until the receptionist at the Jungian Institute in San Francisco told me I was too young and to come back when I was 50 years old. I was heartbroken and cried a lot that night.

But now I find myself studying metaphysics and feeling quite at home with it all. I've learned that the intellectual and spiritual movements of the early 20th century were influenced by such writer and thinkers as Ralph Waldo Emerson and Henry David Thoreau (the Transcendentalists), Bill W and Dr. Bob (of Recovery), Carl Jung, William James, Ernest Holmes, Emma Curtis Hopkins, Aldous Huxley and other. This intellectual and spiritual zeitgeist of the time changed the thinking in the fields of metaphysics, religion, and psychology. Clearly the time was ripe for this new spiritual focus in Western Thought. They are all pointing to a similar source of knowledge and wisdom that we take so for granted today.

I feel so very thankful that my experience and understanding of this wisdom is readily available to me and continues to deepen.

A Near Fatal Car Crash

My husband and I like to take Thursday afternoon and evening to ourselves. We usually drive three hours North on Highway 1 which is a twisty narrow road with breathtaking scenery of the cliffs and ocean below. We are not in a hurry. I am quite familiar with the route and drive rather rapidly in my car. I love to turn up the radio and share my internal changes of late and to catch-up on Eric's latest thoughts and experiences. It is a time for us to reconnect.

This Thursday Eric's mom, who has Alzheimer's, was with us. The power went out in her home, which in a county 1 1/2 hours North of us. Eric has driven up the night before to get her and have her stay with us for a few days.

We had driven up, had a wonderful dinner with an ocean view at a restaurant we frequented often. We were coming home. It was about 9:30 at night, dark, and I was joking about watching Steven Colbert. We were having a great time. There was a quick turn in the road, typical for that highway, when suddenly there were two bright lights coming right at us. I registered on it and thought "the car in in my lane. Is it swerving to pass another?" I blinked and registered that this was not the case. I thought "No it is coming straight at us. I guess I had better turn off on the right to avoid and accident." I pulled onto a wide shoulder area and the car drove toward us. It seemed to be accelerating. It passed so close we could hear the wind and our car shook. I thought it might hit my driver's side rearview mirror, but it didn't. I honked the horn for a long time. Then I started to shake. I called 911 and reported it.

The sighting of the car and the swerve took only three seconds. It was that fast. After we swerved out of the way and stopped by the side of the road, I felt a new sensation. I felt "held in God's hand." I realized and felt the fact that at each moment in my life I am held by God. If it is my time to go then it is my time to go. If it is my time to live, that is also by God's grace.

Becky, Eric and I talked for a brief time about the near-death car crash then we fell silent for a long time. We had been one second away from having a head-on collision. Had I not swerved, we would all now be dead…

About three months ago I had a dream of that exact scene. I was driving South on that narrow highway and a car suddenly appeared heading straight toward me. What I recall most vividly in my dream and in the actual incident is the brightness of the car's lights facing me. They bore into me relentlessly, not swerving at all but coming straight toward me. In my dream I turned abruptly right into some bushes. In reality I turned right into a short strip of shoulder just wide enough for our one car.

I feel that Divine Intelligence had prepared me for the event. In actuality that entire route is mostly narrow twisty turns with one foot at each side surrounded by tall redwoods. There are VERY FEW shoulders or turn-outs along the entire route. What a blessing that I responded the way I did! What blessing to be alive.

The scene keeps repeating in my mind over and over. That is the case for Eric and Becky also. We are stunned and extremely thankful to be alive! I realize it is not my time to go yet. It is just that simple. As Leslie said in her letter to me after her death "You have more to do…More to offer".

Response Paper on Thomas Troward

The idea I would like to discuss from *The Edinburgh and Dore Lectures on Mental Science* (chapters 12-16) ([19])is from chapter 15: The Soul. Intuition, the faculty of the soul, can be cultivated by meditating upon abstract principles related to a particular subject, and we can employ the imagination to convert intuitive perceptions to individual purposes. We find that intuition presents ideas from Universal Mind to the imagination in essence rather than definite form. The imagination then gives these ideas as clear and definite form relative to the individual purposes.

As I mentioned in class, I frequently receive intuitive hits when I am asleep either in dreams or ideas that are fresh in my mind when I wake up. When I go to sleep at night as I am reviewing the day, giving thanks for all of the wonderful things that have happened and seeing if I owe anyone an "amends," I end with the suggestion that my body is healing, returning to perfect original health. Then I say I am falling into a deep sleep and am open to guidance from the Divine through dreams or intuition.

When I awake if there is an idea or concept that pops into my consciousness, I pay attention to it. I figure out if there are some specific things I need to do, which often there are very specific actions I can take in my life to follow the guidance I have received. In this way I am tuning into the Divine a little bit more each day.

After reading the quote above I see that my habits before falling asleep are focusing on aspects of Divine Mind: namely health, guidance, and connection.

I have been amazed over the past year as I have studied Science of Mind and applying the concepts presented, how more focused my mind is upon the intention of aligning with Divine attributes. In January, during my first class, Core Concepts, I set the intention of selling books this year (a book I released in September 2018). Since that time, I have been contacted by a publisher, Maple Leaf Publishing, and practically every day I receive an email or phone call leading me in a new direction of social media postings of the book, book signings, and now translation rights into four languages and a short documentary film. I felt led to write the book, it was an accounting of my personal journal of ideas, thoughts, and experiences during my first nine months in Recovery. Divine Principle has manifested a path far greater than anything I could have imagined. Whenever my self-will starts to take over, things fall apart and a greater plan reveals itself. It is awe inspiring.

Our Bloated Nothingness

I am at my husband's 30th High School Reunion. After three hours of meeting strangers, I've reached my limit. The dinner is over and guests are getting loaded and loud as they dance to the music of a band. We are at a bar with a patio in the back for the crown of 300+ attendees to mingle.

I keep thinking about Ralph Waldo Emerson's "bloated nothingness" mentioned in his lectures. That is what I see around me: unconscious people caught up in their stories about themselves, their past activities and seeming importance.

I never did like bars. I never felt comfortable in them. The loud music prohibits any real conversation and the relating seems to be superficial. The Beatles imitation acoustic band here really had the crowd going. Guess it is a good night to "check out" of reality.

However, in sobriety there is no "checking out. Fortunately, I did not for a second feel like drinking. Thank God that compulsion has been lifted. However, I am present and aware and I'd rather be by myself in the car writing and reflecting than feeling isolated staring at strangers bounce around to the band. I am a true introvert.

Thank goodness I brought a meditation book from the Center for Spiritual Living. How refreshing to open it up and read. I already feel centered again. In it I read:

This is a great reminder to not settle for the average and to be mindful of what the group mind asserts is normal. Especially in the spiritual realm where we are called to look higher, deeper and more clearly into the nature of things. So that we may remain unconvinced that chaos is inevitable or that ordinary is as high as we may aspire. (by Rev. Edward Viljoen)

    How refreshing and just what I needed to feel sane and comfortable in my own skin again.

Becky

Today there are fires all around me in Northern California. I am writing by candle light.

I have not written about Becky, Eric's mom, very much lately. She has Alzheimer's. We go up to her home and hour and a half's drive both ways at least once a week to take care of her: fill her medication trays, buy groceries, do menus for the week, check on the caregiver's notes, *et cetera*. Almost every day we receive a call from the caregivers with questions or concerns. During the course of the last two year she has gradually gotten more and more afflicted by the disease.

Today she is North in the county where she lives. Yesterday both she and we had power outages. Now neither of us have power. Eric just left to try to get through on the one route out of five that is open to get to her home. She is out of pain medications today and we have the new fentanyl patches and hydromorphone pills for the month. We have no choice but to try to get them to her.

Becky's disease has progressed so that she now has very little short- term memory. When we take her out for a meal, she will decide what she wants and by the time the waitress comes for her order, she will have forgotten it. We have to leave notes up on the walls reminding her to do things like "keep the blinds closed so it does not get too hot in the kitchen" or "do not answer the door at night" or "take your p.m. pill when the alarm goes off." Still we have to call and remind her to do these things.

She is forgetting where she lives now and gets confused when she goes out to have a cigarette. I bought her an identification. bracelet with her name, address, ALZHERIMER'S, plus our phone numbers on it. It helps her. It is time to get her into a home soon for her own safety.

She has caregivers who come each day from 1:00 pm until 6:00 p.m. They prepare meals, give her the medications, take her out to smoke cigarettes (her favorite thing) and socialize with neighbors, or to go to the movies. She wants to get everything she sees. If we go to the grocery store she will put items in the basket even though she has them at home. We have to take them out and people stare at us as though we are being mean to her. She will not remember when we get home what we bought. When we take her out for dinner she will not eat her meal and want desert. In short: she is now the child and we are the parents. This has been a subtle but consistent change especially for the last two years. Fortunately, she has a pleasant nature. Still it is trying to be around.

This is very difficult on my husband, Eric. We are doing all we can to help her but nothings will stop this disease from progressing. We feel helpless. We are now exploring options for 24 hours care which we cannot afford. Most likely she will end up in a care facility for people with memory problems which costs about $6,000 per month. We cannot afford this and she only has Social Security. So, we will need funding from the State. I am starting to look into how we can arrange for that.

As hard as we and the doctors try, she is slipping away. Our task now is to keep her safe. When Eric went up this time to get her she had invited a homeless drug addicted man into her home. This is totally unacceptable! She does not realize he might steal her meds and whatever else there is of value in her home, most of which caregivers have already stolen. She is just trying to help him.

Eric just left to try to reach her with her meds and I am a home writing by candle light. There is no way for him and I to talk because there is no internet for our phones to use. If he can he will try to send a text at some point to let me know how he is doing. Maybe I can go to the Starbuck's coffee shop that has internet tomorrow and charge my cell phone.

Becky will come and stay with us for a few days. This is challenging for Eric and me, but I've gotten more used to it. She likes to watch TV all of the time and smoke outside. I make sure she has lots of good food to eat and liquids to drink. We go out for brunch most days (when there is electricity). I give her the meds and a bath when we change the fentanyl patch.

Becky likes to take pretty things from our home. This is very typical of Alzheimer's patients. She will see a bracelet, ring, glass heart *et cetera* and put it into her purse or bag of clothes. We have talked to her asking her to not do this and it stops for a while, but it always comes back. We go through her things before we leave to take her home and pull out most of the things she grabbed. If I don't mind her having it, I let her take it home.

Thank goodness I am in Recovery! I know I my heart and soul I am not alone. I am safe and held in unconditional love and support no matter what the external circumstances of my life may be.

The sun is setting. I pray for safety and comfort for all of the people affected by the fires. Over 200,000 people have been evacuated and most of Northern California, where we live, is without power. About 157 structures have burned and 57 of those were homes. I am blessed to be in my home tonight. God bless us all.

Still Fires

Day four of the fires in our area, Northern California. There are fires all around us. We can see the flames and smell the smoke. We live in Sonoma County in Northern California. It is an emergency situation. Still, I feel calm. My sponsor texted me and I got in touch with my sponsees, such is the support and connection in Recovery. We are all o.k. I misplaced my cell phone which was turned off so I am not sure how I will find it. Last night I was kept awake by some electrical devices calling out "low battery…low battery." I discovered this morning it is the hand held phone, which we have five of. So, I took out the batteries. They will recharge when we get electricity back.

There are 3,500 fire fighters battling the blaze. I found an emergency radio that Leslie bought years ago. I have had it sitting in my office window facing toward the sun to charge the solar batteries for years. It is my only source of information about what is going on. Over a million and a half people are displaced or without electricity. This may last two weeks.

I am keeping up with my routines: morning prayer and meditation and a five mile walk in the morning around the lake (with mask on of course). The air quality is very bad. I only saw a handful of people on my walk when normally there are a dozen or more.

We still have running hot water thanks to a generator on our neighborhood well and gas water heater. I just took a hot shower which felt great! I practically feel normal again.

I was able to buy ice and sandwich makings at the one grocery store in the area that is open so we will have plenty of food to eat. We have lots of bottled water as that is what we usually drink. We have a cooler to keep these few items cool. The refrigerator and freezers cannot be opened. Food can last for a few days. After that, it all has to be thrown out.

There is much to be thankful for. We are still home sleeping in our bed while most people are on cots in shelters. It is 72 degrees in the afternoons which heats up the house. However, it is getting nearly freezing at night and we cannot have a fire in the wood stove because of the poor air quality. So, we bundle up.

A neighbor called on me yesterday which was very reassuring. One neighbor has a home generator for their home, they have a baby to keep warm. I will buy one as soon as they are available again. I've had enough. The last great fire here was in 2017. It looks like it might be an annual event thanks to global warming.

I am enjoying this moment of peace. Fear is all around. Faith is the antidote.

God is my strength… God is my protection…
God is my strength… God is my protection…
God is my strength… God is my protection…
God is my strength… God is my protection…
God is my strength… God is my protection…
God is my strength… God is my protection…

Spiritual Guidance and Discernment

As I mentioned earlier, I go to bed asking for Divine Guidance. Lately what has been happening is that I have been receiving emails about my book from unexpected sources. One, in French, was from a film producer in France interested in doing a film about my book. I have had exchanges with him and we are moving forward on this project. Yesterday I received an email from someone about a radio interview. That felt right also so I moved ahead with it. Some emails do not feel right and I decline the offers that are coming regarding my first book. I believe that God is in charge of this project and it will unfold as it should if I just use discernment.

This can be very subtle. In the publishing industry I am finding there is an emphasis on ego. They want to appeal to my ego and to promote me, the author. I reemphasize that I am anonymous and that the book is not about me. The book is about the reality of a spiritual life available to all of us if we let go and give our life to the Divine. Some do not understand this and I refuse to deal with these people. The book is an act of service.

What I am trying to describe is the feeling that the book is unfolding as it should. God is in charge of this. And my job is to stay out of the way. I trust that I am being guided and receive much help in the classes that I am currently taking at the Center for Spiritual Living. They currently are discussing just this topic.

To stay centered I keep doing my familiar daily routines. The morning prayers and meditation center me. Then the two-hour walk around the lake brings me serenity. I love stopping at the same bench each day and seeing the same serene view of the lake, the reeds on the side, ducks and geese swimming by, and the hills reflected in the lake. How soothing it is that as my life changes there is stillness and steadiness at that bench. It is untouched by my affairs.

About two months ago I was saying I had no friends. I am noticing that now invitations are coming in for me to join a women's group, speak at a meeting, go for coffee… Clearly the universe has said "yes" to my desire to have close women friends in my life. I simply needed to be open to seeing the possibilities.

When I was reading *The Sermon on the Mount* by Emmet Fox about ten months ago, I was struck by a paragraph about "Give us this day our daily bread." Emmet Fox was expanding that this refers not only to the bread we eat, but to all that we need in life: friends, family, inspiration, books, finances, work, and so forth. He noted that our lives should be interesting. That struck me because at the time my life was not active and interesting enough for me. Now it is. I simply needed to open to and accept the invitations that were all around.

The sermon the week after the fires ended was about gratitude. How important it is to focus on gratitude especially when we are feeling overwhelmed by life's challenges. Some suggest doing a gratitude list daily for a month. The point is that as we notice things to be grateful for, we attract them to us. This is called the Law of Attraction. How important it is to pay attention to what we are thinking.

Scientific Christian: Mental Practice By Emma Curtis Hopkins [20]

This powerful book is life changing. It emphasis certain attitudes and practices that, if done consistently, will change the life of the Science of Mind Practitioner and touch those around them.

Here are a few quotes that have meaning to me:

God is omnipotent, omnipresent, and omniscient.

In God I live and move and have my being.

The I AM works through me to will and to do that which ought to be done by me.

Mind will demonstrate as much greatness as it has courage to stand by its intention.

I am to keep the words of truth going within me continuously.

I must give up guilt (belief in personal sin or wrongdoing) and blame (the belief in sin or wrongdoing of others).

I must pronounce myself as a spiritual being with spiritual powers to heal.   .

Emma Curtis Hopkins speaks of a living, vibrant and personal experience of the Divine NOW. She reassuringly tells us we will be given the strength and guidance to do that which is ours to do. Our task is to constantly mind our thoughts to not accept any doubt or blame for ourselves or others. Then the Good within each of us will be manifest.

These are ideas to be savored and practiced throughout a whole lifetime. This is a goal to aspire to. It is a map toward union with God, feeling God's presence within and around us, and resonating the Truth so that others respond in kind with health and wholeness.

Spiritual Roots of Science of Mind

In this class I have felt seen, affirmed, challenged and guided. The readings were deep and challenging. It was taught by Reverend Ruth Barnhart whom I like very much. Our class discussions were helpful to put the readings into the context of our own lives. There are specific ideas from each author that have been useful to me.

- Useful thoughts from Ralph Waldo Emerson: [18]
- We experience the Infinite only to the degree that It expresses Itself through us, becoming to us that which we believe it to be.
- Prayer is the contemplation of facts from the highest point of view.
- *"Bloated Nothingness"* is the false evaluation which we place upon things.
- Spirituality is the atmosphere of God's Presence, Goodness, Truth and Beauty.
- We live in the eternal now.
- Our faith comes in glimpses and our vices are habitual.
- Useful thoughts from Thomas Troward: [19]
- A seed thought – an idea or concept that is focused on every day and I observe how I see the Divine moving it along in my life.
- The distinctive power of Spirit is thought, the distinctive power of Matter is form.

- The subjective mind is the organ of the Absolute and the objective mind is the organ of the Relative.
- We understand our projections by seeing what dynamics keep appearing on our lives.
- We should not limit our expectations of the future c
- There is Primary Cause, subjective and unconscious mind, and Secondary Cause, consciousness, intellectual mind, time and space.
- Form a clear concept in the objective mind of the idea we wish to convey to the subjective mind.
- The basis of all healing is a change in belief.
- The Universal Mind is always to us exactly what we believe it to be.
- Useful thoughts from Emma Curtis Hopkins: [20]
- God is omnipotent, omnipresent, and omniscient.
- In God I live and move and have my being.
- The I AM works through me to will and to do that which ought to be done by me.
- Mind will demonstrate as much greatness as it has courage to stand by its intention.
- I am to keep the words of truth going within me continuously.
- I must give up guilt (belief in personal sin or wrongdoing) and blame (the belief in sin or wrongdoing of others).
- I pronounce myself as a spiritual being with spiritual powers to heal.

Thanksgiving

It is Thanksgiving. This is a special day in America, a national holiday, where we gather together as families to eat turkey, dressing, cranberry sauce, and pumpkin pie to celebrate the first meal between the settlers and Indians, supposedly. It is a "family" holiday and can bring up a lot of feelings for most people.

This year we found out late that both caregivers were taking off the week to be with their families. That meant that Eric would go up to take care of Becky for five days. I was not too thrilled about that. We discussed it and agreed that he would come back on Friday after the Thursday Thanksgiving to give us a day together. That felt o.k. to both of us.

Last night I decided to go to the choir celebration at the Center for Spiritual Living. It was wonderful, very uplifting. The other day as I was on my walk, I noticed two cars that are frequently parked along my route that probably contain homeless men. They are allowed to stay the night in the park with a pass obtained upon entrance to the park. I decided to get a box lunch from Kentucky Fried Chicken for each one and drop it off which I did and it was great fun. I met on man, Pete, and his cat. The other did not leave his van to get the food so I left if on his windshield. It felt good to think of others. I also heard from my sponsor and sponsees.

I am feeling very thankful at this moment. I got an email from the wife of the film produced in France who wants to turn my book into a film, saying how much she liked my new video by Carol O'Dell on my website. She said it made her cry. It made me cry also. Although I wrote it, it was delivered with such sensitivity and the story is so dear that it made me cry. How blessed I am to have lived this experience!

A Dinner Party

My last class at the Center for Spiritual Living has ended and, as usual, I find myself feeling a bit restless. I have decided to have a dinner party, which I oftentimes do in between classes. I plan to invite around six people which makes eight with Eric and I, a nice size. I think everyone will enjoy each other's company as most do not yet know each other.

I enjoy having dinner parties. It was a bit difficult for me at first when I became sober but I have found that good discussions, sparkling cyder and delicious food make for a fun evening for me. I plan to use Leslie's mother's china from France which is white with a gold ring around it which will be festive for the holidays. Over the years I have collected lots of china, silver place settings, table cloths and cloth napkins, crystal wine glasses and serving dishes. The table always looks wonderful. This is how my mother used to set the dinner table for guests and for holidays so it feels comfortable for me. To my surprise, many have not had this experience. But most seem to enjoy the elegance and feel spoiled by having it.

I have the menu planned, a simple anti-pasta plate followed by lasagna with a green salad and garlic French bread then sorbet and chocolates for dessert. I love to cook and my lasagna always gest rave reviews. I have found the most awkward part of the evening can be after dessert. What to do or talk about? Instead of brandy, I propose a topic for discussion. At the last dinner party, the topic was "a favorite book," which I thought would be easy because I love to read. However, I discovered some at the dinner did not enjoy reading so it was difficult for them to answer. This time it will be "to recall a few of the most wonderful moments of the past year." That should end it.all on an upbeat note. I'll write more about this after the event.

I have invited the guests and am awaiting the rsvp's. I look forward to the event in two weeks on a Sunday evening at 6:00 p.m.

A Christmas Tree

Eric came home unannounced this afternoon with a Christmas Tree. We had not discussed buying one, it just showed up along with two wreaths, 50 feet of garland for the outside porch railings, and honey covered peanuts. He was delighted. I was not.

This is just another example of him showing up with stuff for our home without talking to me about it. I feel crowded out of my own home. He insisted it would fit into the living room and after moving all of the furniture around, it did.

hile he was doing this, I was feeling claustrophobic and a knot was forming in my stomach. I felt like there was not an inch of space left anymore for me in my own home, that he has totally taken over. I burst into tears. What seemed to him to be a wonderful festive activity felt like a violation to me. We tried to talk about it but will need to pick it up with the therapist tomorrow.

Leslie, my wife and life partner of twenty years died on December 27 five years ago. Each Christmas has been a dreaded time for me. I try to get through the holidays with as little disruption to my normal routine as possible. For me it is a painful time and this was exasperated by having stuff brought into my home further invading my space. Eric said he is dealing with his feelings of loss by buying things, stuffing down his feelings, and trying to enjoy the holidays. I feel like emotionally disconnecting from the whole thing. We couldn't be farther apart in our reactions.

Instead of feeling uplifted I feel thrust into my grief for Leslie. I feel a sense of deep loss. Five years ago, Leslie was on her death bed upstairs hanging onto life. She died at 3:00 a.m. on December 27, 2014. I was sleeping next to her and woke up when she had her last breath. It was a terrible time for me.

I was trying to let in the holiday spirit and even lighted a pine scented candle last night that Eric had bought for me trying to get into the spirit of things. Now the deep grief has surfaced again. I feel raw. Tears are streaming down my face. The grief is back full force. I haven't felt this bad since two Christmases ago when Amy, my sponsor, comforted me. I am not being comforted. I am being confronted with her loss. The thought of hanging up the Christmas ornaments, hand painted glass ones from Germany that I bought for her one each year, just makes me feel her loss more. I feel deep grief that hurts my heart.

Eric keeps repeating how much he loves this season and wants to celebrate. He keeps hanging up ornaments around the house. I don't know what to do. I want to go for a walk but it is late and dark and cold outside.

I can only wait for relief to come. I guess this is part of my healing process.

We saw our therapist, Peter, and he pointed out that right now I need stability in my life. I need for nothing to change.

A Tree Fell

Last night in the 50 mile an hour winds and rain a pine tree in my front yard broke, fell, and tore down all cable lines to my home and my neighbor's home which in turn caught the edge of our gutters on the front of the house which in turn fell down onto the top of the carport. Thank God I just had the carport built or it would have totally damaged my Mercedes. I am so upset I cannot sleep.

This morning at 9:00 a.m. the neighbor woke me up yelling at me about how outraged she was by my neglect of the tree and what an immense inconvenience it is to her to be without her internet access for four days. I have been trying to get the tree taken down for the last three weeks. I had PG&E out but their said it wasn't touching their wires so it was the landlord's problem. I had my landscaper out who said he would send me a quote. Well it was not taken care of in time and now we have this mess.

I have contacted the appropriate authorities to fix the lines and file a homeowner's claim for the damages. So, things will get taken care of in time. I wrote my neighbor an apology card enclosing $250.00 cash to compensate for her inconvenience which made her feel better.

But what has surfaced louder than anything is the fact that five years ago on December 27, 2014 my life partner and wife of twenty years Leslie died of cancer. I had been barely holding onto my center but with all of the turmoil of late the grief had come crashing into my consciousness. I just went to the service at the Center for Spiritual Living and cried all of the way through it. I went to a prayer treatment afterward and then saw my instructor Rev. Ruth who comforted me and reminded me that grief comes in waves and that I need to be gentle with myself, that it will pass. That is the only thing that makes sense right now: that I am in deep grief once again and just need to get through it as best as I can and be gentle with myself in the process. I feel exhausted from crying and handling problems in my life and with Eric's mother who has Alzheimer's. I have no energy to do anything so will go to bed to rest. I will log onto the CSL website to sign up for a new class in January which will lift my spirits. Then I will take a nap.

I awoke feeling rested and in touch with my very tender heart. I decided to rent and watch the movie *Harold and Maude*. Harold represents the emptiness that is felt by a sensitive young man who is surrounded by a superficial reality. He tries desperately to communicate to his mother his sense of hopelessness by staging fake suicides, which she ignores and deals with in inappropriate ways. Maude represents the zest for life that someone close to death can understand. It is about real issues that I understand. I like it.

I know part of my sorrow is that Eric is gone so much at his mom's. He has spent eight of the last twelve days up there, is up there now, and will spend four of the next seven days up there. I hope we can get her placed into a home in the new year.

A Dream

I just awoke from a very deep sleep and a dream. In my dream I was back in the College Town living in the little house that my parents bought for me to live in while I was doing my Bachelor's and Master's work. I was not in the home but looking behind it at the white garage of the owner of the larger property I was a part of. They were a quiet retired couple. I lived in the country. I was happy there. In fact, it was one of the happiest times of my life, living alone, going to school, studying Ju Jitsu and working at Tower Records. In my dream I thought: "why did I even leave? I would have been happy there. Why didn't I just stay there?" But it was not enough at the time. For some reason I have kept pushing myself onward toward more. Why is that? More is not the answer.

At that time, I had very little money. I remember I could not afford tomatoes at the store. I lived on $250.00 a month including rent to my parents. Still, I was happy. I was in touch with myself. I was putting myself through college on a Pell Grant, a scholarship, and working the six to midnight shift at Tower Records. Chico is in the valley in California which means that the summers are hot, in the 100's. I fondly remember bicycling home after work on warm summer evenings. I felt safe and content bicycling through the town at night. I was at peace.

Now I find myself wanting to simplify and go inward. I am looking forward to my next class at the Center for Spiritual Living on daily spirituality. I will be reading *Journey of Awakening: A Meditator's Guidebook* by Ram Dass and *Can We Talk to God?* by Ernest Holmes. I have already ordered them so I can start reading now. I feel adrift when I am not in a class at the Center. I seem to be happiest now again living simply, going inward.

I have been a seeker. I am seeking to know and experience life. Where does this come from? I am always pushing. I awake each morning, get out of bed, grab a protein bar and drive to the park to walk five miles around the lake. I do this every day knowing that if I don't, I will be disappointed with myself for not going and will probably not sleep well that night either. I seem to be "programmed" to push myself!

The Dinner Party

We had the dinner party and it was the best one I have ever had. It was such a delightful combination of people who all got along so well together. I have never laughed so much. Most were in Recovery and the last person did not mind that we had sparkling cider instead of wine (some people do and I don't invite them over now, maybe later). One guest is a musician and when he saw my 1935 restored Chickering Baby Grand piano he just had to play it much to all of our entertainment. On the table in the living room I had a Christmas orchid that had just bloomed. It was gorgeous and very special. It only blooms every other year.

At the end of the dinner, I asked each person to share some favorite memories from 2019. What a wonderful way to get people to open their hearts to one another! We all found out things about each other that we had not known before.

I realized that this year I have been able to form new friendships that are very dear to me and to Eric. What a gift that is in life! I had been feeling a lack of friends and recall talking about it to Frances in therapy. Thanks to my dinner parties, going to the Center for Spiritual Living, and Recovery we have found people we have a lot in common with. Everyone expressed appreciation for my dinner parties which surprised me. My mother taught me how to be a good hostess and I so appreciate that side of myself. It takes about two weeks for me to plan and execute a dinner party. I prepare the food and set the table the day before so I can enjoy the beauty of the fine china, silver and crystal that I have. It is a joy to look at and everyone always comments on it. It is a way for me to spoil my friends for an evening.

I usually thrown a dinner party between my classes at the Center for Spiritual Living. During my ten-week classes I am so busy with homework and class that I do not have the time and energy to do it. But when the class ends, I seem to always feel a loss and throwing a dinner party is just the thing to raise my spirits. What a blessing that I can now relax while doing so. I used to have so much social anxiety that I drank a lot. Now I feel comfortable with myself and others and able to just stay in the moment and experience it all unfolding. I have given up my need to control which feel so much better!

Christmas

Today is Christmas. I have had the most wonderful two days.

Last night, Christmas Eve, we went to the Candle Lighting Service at the Center for Spiritual Living. It was just what I had hoped it would be and more. As a child we always went to the Candle Light Service at the Lutheran Church after a delicious Swedish dinner prepared by my mom. This year, there was a chorus and orchestra of about 50 people. It sounded very professional and moving. We started by singing some Christmas carols then the orchestra and chorus took over. There was a sermon by Rev. Edward. He discussed the many holy days that occur at this time of year: the lighting of the lamps of the Menorah, a Jewish tradition; winter solstice; and of course, the birth of Jesus in the Christian tradition. All of these celebrate the coming of the light after the darkness of the longest day of the year. They also celebrate the Divine Love that is present and available in each moment. At the end of the service each person was invited to come up front and light a candle from the Center Candle. As we did this, we were to reflect of what we were lighting our candle for. I lite mine in honor of brining the Divine Love into my heart more fully in the coming year. The entire service was so moving that I cried throughout. The presence of the Divine was palpable. My heart was opened with the joy of receiving it. Then we all sang Silent Night and Joy to the World.

Today we went to the early morning service. We had Spiritual Mind Treatments and reflections on the reality of the Divine Loving Presence available to us each moment. We reflected on, as it saying in *A Course in Miracles*, [12] that each of us is either extending love or calling for it. How hard it is to remember this when the other person is hiding their love behind layers.of hurt, pain, and suffering and lashing out at us in pain. Their call for love often feels like an attack, as it may be. However, our task is to realize that and remember the tender loving soul beneath all of the pain. We sang Christmas Carols and greeted one another.

What a blessing it is to be able to gather and have these rituals. They are moving and very powerful. Not everyone in the world is allowed to do this. Yet they find their own secret ways to worship. It is in our nature to remember and long for the Light in the Darkness. May I remember this all year long!

My Support System

I have come to realize that I have a support system that keeps me balanced, feeling loved and loving, and spiritually nourished. Most important, upon awakening I turn my will and life over to God. This reestablishes the new basis of my reality – trusting in and resting in my Higher Power each moment of the day. Next, I go for my five mile walk around the lake. Here I routinely see friends I have come to know who have the same habit. We don't usually stop to talk but just say "hi" in a friendly sort of way. I feel connected to others.

Then I go to breakfast at a restaurant in town that is frequented by locals. It is owned by an extended Mexican family and it feels like I have become one of them. They ask where Eric, my husband, is if not along, which has been quite a lot lately. Due to problems with caregivers for his mom taking off time for the holidays he has only been home five days this month, so I am getting used to him being gone. It has been good for me to get in touch with myself again. I find I am doing more spiritual reading and meditation with him gone. I plan to continue this practice and am starting a new class on medication soon.

I come home from breakfast and work on this book, answer emails about my first book and take care of things. I try to find time to watch the PBS Newshour each day to keep up on current events even though there seems to be so much turmoil in the world.

In the evenings I often go to a Recovery meeting or to a class at the Center for Spiritual Living. I find emotional support there from many new friends. I also offer support to newcomers remembering well my fears and trepidation when first walking through those doors.

Tonight, I have been asked to share at a Recovery meeting my experience, strength and hope. I look forward to this opportunity. I have changed so much for the better and love life now when before I was suicidal. I received an email from a friend who is not in Recovery saying that psychotherapy and antidepressants are an answer to alcoholism. I wrote back saying that had not worked for me and I would not go back to drinking for anything. It shocked me that he would suggest it. I think he is considering it for himself as he is in Recovery and smokes marijuana a lot which is just escaping from reality. It made me realize how joyful I am about this new life. For me, the spiritual path is my answer. I get help from suggestions and sharing from others as well as from books and classes. I now feel in the presence must of the time and when I am out of it, it is obvious by my anxiety and emotional suffering. I try to get back to center, as I call it, as soon as possible.

No one could have explained to me in my darkest hours the joyful path that would unfold for me. I was convinced I was through having anything to offer to this world when I walked into Recovery. That gift of desperation facilitated my willingness to do all that was suggested to me to turn away from alcohol and learn a new way of living. Today is full of hope and promise. When the structure of my previous life fell away (retired from career; my wife of twenty years, Leslie, died and I was swallowed up in grief and sadness; the house was nearly destroyed by a water heater leak and had to be rebuilt from the inside out…) I realized I had nothing to stand on. I turned to alcohol which is not my friend but rather took me down deeper and deeper into despair.

I think this is why I can so appreciate every little piece of my day which gives me meaning today. Each part is a unique gift from the universe. I am so grateful and would not change it for the world. I am expecting more goodness and service to unfold each day. I belong and am a part of the solution not the problem. I have found that I am a spiritual being having a physical experience. I am no longer defined by my externals. I am defined by my internal walk with the Divine. This is a priceless gift!

The New Year

A New Year has begun. Some people set goals for themselves in the beginning of a new year. They usually do not come true. Why is this? I think it is because they create a picture of the future based upon ideals about themselves that are not yet real. They imagine a new personality or way of coping with life as if that can magically happen. I would like to suggest another approach: using intention. Goals are in the future, while intentions are present tense.

It is so important that we train our minds to feed them with the thoughts we want to guide our lives. The most fruitful way to do that is by accepting into our lives that which we want to attract. In other words, instead of saying "I will have friends" you say to yourself "I have friends." That simple switch moves the focus from something that will be attained in the future (when I will be happy, fulfilled, *et cetera*) to the present. The task then becomes to notice and appreciate the friends that are in your life and are coming into your life.

I did this a year ago. I was aware that I had changed so much that my old friends, except a few, no longer seemed to share my current interests and way of seeing the world and I wanted to create a new network of friends, a new social fabric for myself. I started asking myself to notice when I met someone if I felt a sense of connection with them. If so, I started to pursue conversations with them. This included people in Recovery meetings, at my church, during my walks around the lake each morning. Then I took the big step of inviting them to my home for small dinner parties which can allow for further deepening of connection and mutual understanding. This took a lot of courage on my part. I was still unfamiliar with entertaining without alcohol being involved. Still I prepared the menu and reminded myself that the purpose of the event was to simply enjoy new people in my life; that I could relax and let the event unfold. I served sparkling cider instead of wine and found that the evenings went quite well. I've added peaceful mediation music quietly going on in the background which helps me to relax and I believe helps my guests relax as well. The conversation does indeed carry the evening and we all have a great time.

Intention involves mentally stating what we want to manifest in our lives and then noticing when these things show up and then building on that, following the path. This means being in the present moment, paying attention and responding. It also involves trust rather than force. I don't force my will upon myself and others, I listen with my intuition to the guidance that I receive. It is getting into the flow of life rather than forcing it to my will.

Divine Love

God is love. All religions teach this. But what kind of love is it? I think I have an idea. When I was sixteen years old getting ready for a Modern Dance Concert at my High School, my mother was sewing some fabric onto my tights and leotard in the atrium in our home. It was a hot Saturday afternoon. I fainted and hit my head on a rock. What I experienced was my body floating above my physical body, on my back with my feet first. It was dark all around me but I wasn't scared. I was rather curious. I saw a speck of light way ahead and started floating toward it. As I got closer to the light, I felt an unconditional love I had never known on this earth. I knew I was returning home and wanted to stay there. There were beings of light around me. I was thinking about some bad behaviors in my life and I felt them reassure me that I had done nothing wrong, rather, that they understood what I was trying to do and understood and then encouraged me to love myself. I then heard my mother and sister calling me and awoke on the living room couch surrounded by them and the family doctor. I had been out about a half hour.

I never told anyone about this experience realizing that it was unusual, other worldly. Years later when I was working at Tower Books and Records I saw the book *Near Death Experiences* by Raymond Moody. I read it and realized that was what I had experienced. This was reassuring.

I believe that this is Divine Love. I expericnce it when I pray to turn my will and life over to my Higher Power. I experienced it when I was at the Candlelight Service this year and it made me cry. It is such a sweetness. It fills my heart.

I think I need to meditate on this sweetness. I need to practice devotion to fill.my heart and increase my awareness of this goodness. I also need to apply it to myself and others, to not judge. This can be very challenging. I am working on it.

Spiritual Mind Treatment To Release Worry

One of the changes I have noticed in my life is how I deal with troubling situations. When I realize I have confusion or worry about a situation or person, I try to identify the God quality of the solution and do a Spiritual Mind Treatment for it. For example, recently I have been concerned about the direction for this book: how to proceed, which publisher to go with, who to contact for help. I immediately did a Treatment for my confusion.

Purpose: Clarity about how to proceed with publishing this book.

Recognition: Spirit is present now. It is the Source of all creation: the beauty of the forests, the majesty of the oceans, the clouds, the untold universes that swirl around in perfect orbit. This Source holds and sustains all that exists.

Unification: I am an individualized expression of the Divine. In God I live and move and have my being. I am guided and led to all that I need in life. I am united with this Spirit.

Realization: I know that I have clarity about how to proceed with the publishing of this manuscript. I am guided by the Divine Spirit to fulfill my work on this earth. I am a servant of the Divine. I rest and move and have my being in Source. I am able to discern the direction for my book: who to talk to about it, how to proceed. I release all worry. I claim clarity and peace.

Thanksgiving: I know that the Law of Life has acted upon my words and it is already done. I give thanks for the reality of Spirit in my life. I am blessed.

Release: I simply let go, get God, and rest assured that all is well.

And so it is.

Then I let go and go about my day. I am sensitive to the leading of Spirit in my life. Sunday in service I was led to ask Rev. Edward Viljoen about my publishing questions. He is a published author and spiritual guide so I thought he would be a good person to ask. He did give me feedback which was useful and a website for more guidance. I received a call from an agent wanting to represent me so I sent that person this draft and a synopsis of the book. I now rest in the assurance that all is unfolding as it should.

This shift from worry to Spiritual Mind Treatment has been profound. I find that instead of focusing on a problem I am switching my attention to the solution to that problem and to God. It makes my life my easier. I feel more peace.

Spiritual Mind Treatment for Forgiveness

I am learning in my class Treatment and Meditation how to do affirmative prayer treatment for others. This week the assignment was to do a treatment for a prayer partner. In class she discussed with me how her anger was keeping her down spiritually, that she was learning to forgive and it was setting her free. I wrote a treatment for her to continue in this direction.

To release anger and feel forgiveness.

Recognition: There is One Divine Presence. It is Love. It is in all things seen and unseen. It is in the stars and planets displayed in the night sky. It is in the plants, trees, animals, fish, majestic mountains, awesome oceans. It is ever present, all powerful and all knowing.

Unification: I am connected to this Presence. It flows through me as me in every moment. As this is true for me it is true for my prayer partner. She is an individualized expression of the Divine, perfect and whole.

Realization: I speak my word for her. I declare that she releases all anger and judgement of herself and others. She naturally lets go of these feelings and accepts forgiveness in her heart. She feels a healing in her heart and soul for all perceived wrongs of the past. She lets them go and lets in Light, Love, and Wholeness. She is free from the past. She lives in the present moment aware of God's Presence in herself and others. She is healed.

Thanksgiving: For this shift in consciousness I give thanks. I realize it has already happened. It is done.

Release: So I simply let it go.

And so it is.

Moss and Ferns

I went for my morning walk around the lake today. I had not been there for four days due to rain and commitments to Recovery and the Center for Spiritual Learning.

I was struck by the beauty of the scenery. The rain had prompted a gorgeous layer of moss to grow on the trees and forest floor. Small ferns had sprung up among the dried leaves and moss. The forest looked alive and magical.

Geese were calling loudly announcing themselves. It is mating season. They are finding mates, establishing territory and making nests. In April and May, the fruits of their union will burst forth. Flocks of yellow puff balls will appear following around their mother and pecking at the grass. I will watch as they grow during the Fall.

How wonderous to observe nature, to notice it where before I had just walked by absorbed in my thoughts. I've come to realize my walks are a meditation. They are a time to notice nature and calm my active mind. I stop half way through the walk at a bench I call the "serenity bench." The scene is always the same: the lake so peaceful and serene with clouds and ducks, surrounding trees reflected in the lake like a mirror. Today there were two mud hens diving down and popping up a few minutes later ten or twenty feet away.

I was blessed to grow up on a lake. I had many days and hours to explore nature. It was in Oregon which is very wet and lush. The lake where I walk now reminds me of that time.

It's strange how my life had passed so quickly, at least, that is how it feels now. At the time though there were many hardships to endure and learn from..

    I am so thankful for this phase of my life. I have time to reflect and enjoy life, to notice and help others. I enjoyed that part of teaching college students, helping them with their personal struggles. I get to do that now with my sponsees and in treating for others from the Center for Spiritual Living. It feels good to give. I feel like the moss and ferns: so full of life that I have some to give away. There is an abundance of energy and grace.

    I saw one tree blooming. It had little white flowers on it that looked like little lanterns, about thirty in a bunch throughout the tree branches. It looked like nature had decorated the tree with light.

    I feel blessed, and peaceful.

Thursdays

Thursdays are my favorite day of the week. It is the day that Eric and I take off for ourselves to be together. In the early afternoons we leave to drive up the coast. The highway is windy and goes along the beautiful Pacific Ocean. I love to drive along the twisty roads driving as fast as I can in my car which handles so well and hugs the road on every turn. I manage to stay in the right lane most of the time but sometimes drift over to the wrong side of the road for a brief moment.

It takes a half hour to get from our home to the coast. We pass over gorgeous rolling hills with fields of green grass, ranches with cows and sheep, old windmills and picturesque farm houses. Then we dip down to the ocean, smell the salty air, and see the first waves rolling in. It is at this point that I always think about the many Thursday afternoons for thirty years that I sat behind a desk looking at a computer screen doing emails, analyzing data and writing reports. I then feel the freedom of the open road ahead and a sense of adventure with what lies ahead: three hours of open road, the ocean to my left as we head up North to a small town where we stop for dinner. During dinner we sit and look at the ocean, the fishing boats coming in from a day's catch, the seals swimming in the harbor, sea gulls flying by, the sun setting into the bay.

Driving back Eric drives and I get to look at the scenery. I notice the large ranches with cows and sheep and horses wandering freely on the hillsides. Along the road are redwoods hundreds of years old stretching up seventy feet high into the air. Moss and ferns frame the highway. Deer, foxes, skunks and mice run across the road. Sometimes we see large hawks on the telephone wires peering down at us. Tonight, there was a half-moon shining on the ocean illuminating the waves and the cliffs below.

Most of the time we have the radio on. We are in the moment enjoying the pleasure of free time together. We listen to a satellite station that plays music from the '70s. We sing along to *Into the Mystic* by Van Morrison, *You've Got a Friend* by Carole King and other favorites by the Doobie Brothers, James Taylor, Gordon Lightfoot, the Rolling Stones and many others. Our minds drift and we share thoughts we've had during the week, what has moved us, what we are concerned with, the joys and sorrows.

It is time apart from all worries and concerns of daily life. There is no cell phone service so we are not interrupted. I feel just in the present moment, aware of the curve in the road, the clouds in the sky, the ocean waves below. It renews me. I feel peace and gratitude. I am blessed.

Spiritual Mind Treatment To Be True To Oneself

Purpose: For my prayer partner to identify her feelings, journal about them, and be true to herself in thought and action.

Recognition: One Spirit is present now. It flows in and through all that exists, all that is manifest and unmanifest. It has always been, is present now, and will always be. It is a force for Good. It is a force for fulfillment, clarity, consciousness and unification. It is all knowing, always providing guidance and lighting the path before us. It is for us. It has all power. There is no lack in Spirit.

Unification: I am one with the awesome force. It is my source, my expression, my life. I consciously unite with the Power for Good in all my actions and thoughts. And as this is so for me it is so for her.

Realization: She feels the welling up of feelings that guide her in her life to understand life's circumstances and make wise choices for herself. She trusts this Spirit, has faith in its ever-present guidance, trusts and follows her feelings. She takes time daily to turn inward and discern her feelings, to notice her reactions to life, to honor her inner guidance. She trusts and follows this inner knowing, writes about it daily in her journal, and applies these new insights into her life. She is creating a new life path for herself based upon self-knowledge, self-trust, and self-regard.

Thanksgiving: For this awareness in her, for her desire to change and move her life in this new direction, I give thanks for I know it has already taken place in Spirit. The Law has acted upon new feelings and insights and she rests in peace as a life of harmony for her unfolds.

Release: Knowing that the Word has been spoken and the Law has acted upon it, I rest in complete confidence that it is done. I release this Prayer and let God.

Spiritual Mind Treatment For Surgery

Purpose: For Eric to know that his sister's surgery will go well, that she will live through it.

Recognition: The is One Infinite Divine Love at the very center and through all that exists. This Power and Intelligence created this magnificent world and the expansion of the universes that stretch beyond our comprehension.

Unification: This same wisdom flows through us, guiding and nurturing us at every moment. I know that I am united with this force, this intelligence, it has made me and breathes me every second of my life. It continues after the death of this physical body. I am a Spirit having a human experience. And as this is true for me it is true for Eric and her. In God we live and move and have our being. There is no where we can go where God is not present, holding us in Its Loving Embrace.

Realization: I claim for Eric a new emergence of this knowledge, a peace and tranquility of the Loving Guidance that lights his way every second of every day. Eric feels a certainty in his mind and heart and body that God is here with him and with her. In the operating room, God is. In the preparation, in every action during the surgery, in every moment of the

Recovery, God is present. We live and move and have out being in God, in Goodness, in Oneness, in Peace and Wholeness. Our healthy bodies reflect this fact. Our healing reflects this fact. I know that she is increasing in awareness of her Divine Self through this illness. The process is healing her spirit, mind, emotions and body.

Thanksgiving: I give thanks for the completeness of this Treatment. I know the words have been placed into the hands of the Divine Healer and they are being acted upon now and in the future.

Release: All is done so I simply let go and let God.

Spiritual Mind Treatment for Rose

Purpose: For me for the gift that I am in this life.

Recognition: There is One Creative Divine Intelligence that is the Source of all that exists, all that has been and all that will be. That One is God. That Source is unconditional love. It is a force for our Good. It says "yes" to all our thoughts. It creates.

Unification: I am one with this Source. It is the origin of my life ever flowing through me as I cocreate with it to a demonstration of my understanding of it. My thoughts create my body and life experience through God. God is in, around, and through me.

Realization: I realize that I am a unique creation of the Divine. I have a Divine purpose in being on this earth at this time in history. I have unique ways of expressing Good in the world. God moves through me. I am God's voice, God's touch, God's thoughts, God's expression in my writing and speech. Divine Intuition guides me at all times to do that which I am to do and be. I relax into the Love of God and feel serenity and peace, the serenity of my soul.

Thanksgiving: For this recognition I give thanks. For this awareness I am overfilled with gratitude for the reality of Divine Expression through and as me. I thank God for this truth.

Release: Having said my word I know the Law of Life is giving it expression now and in the future.

I simply release and let go and let God.
And so it is.

What is Spiritual Mind Treatment?

The world's great religions agree that there is one creative intelligence that underlies all reality. It is called many different names: God, Allah, Yahweh, Jehovah, First Cause, Chi, Qi, Adonai, Hashem, Krishna, Buddha nature, Tao, the I AM. God is ever present, all knowing, and all powerful. It is power, beauty, light, love, benevolence, kindness, forgiveness, peace, and serenity. It is ever drawing us closer to Itself.

Ernest Holmes distilled this understanding into the Science of Mind philosophy. He states that in the macrocosm the Word, or First Cause, is the origin of all that has ever existed or will exist. It is eternal. Thought proceeds manifestation. In the microcosm humans create their life experiences by their thoughts conscious and unconscious. Most of our deepest thoughts about ourselves come from our family and society and are unconscious. We accept on some level that we are not good enough; that we are inferior because of the color of our skin, our gender, our sexual orientation, our disabilities…that we are not worthy. These thought forms are creating our existence oftentimes beyond our awareness. Therefore, it is essential that we bring to consciousness our assumptions about life and ourselves.

Ernest Holmes and others teach that we can heal ourselves and others through the use of Affirmative Prayer called Spiritual Mind Treatment. In this process the practitioner claims for themselves and the other, the reality of their Divine Existence devoid of illness or lack of any kind.

Emmet Fox in his book *The Sermon on the Mount* [21] states that Jesus taught spiritually or metaphysically. Fox states that serenity is tranquility of the soul. "To pray scientifically means to affirm that God is helping us, that temptation has no power against us, and to constantly claim that our own real nature is spiritual and perfect (p. 55). "

In *The Lord's Prayer* Jesus teaches us to accept each day our daily bread. We are to expect that God will provide us fully with everything we need. "Bread does not merely mean food but all that that we require for a healthy, happy, free, and harmonious life. This includes food, clothing, shelter, means to travel, books, and so on; above all, we require freedom" (Fox, p. 162) [21]. We are free to choose to accept the Divine Goodness or rely on our own self for supply.

Surrender is required in order to experience God's perfect Grace. Most us of surrender a little bit at a time. We may pray in the morning, meditate for a half hour, go to yoga class, and give thanks in the evening. We may experience peace and serenity at these times. Then we go back to our normal experiences of reality, strife, and anxiety. Emerson states "our faith comes in glimpses while our vices are perpetual." We are instructed by Jesus to pray without ceasing. We are to live in the Presence of God every moment of our lives.

For some surrender is complete and sudden. This opening is prompted by a feeling of desperation and the awareness that all that has had meaning in one's life before makes no sense, has led to failure, lack, and often suicidal thoughts. This awareness makes the person open to receive God's Grace and learn a new way of life. It is a gift of desperation that creates a willingness to release our hold on our life and let God take over. There is a shattering of the illusion of separateness and a restoration of the soul to its wholeness.

What are we to do when we experience lack? Joel Goldsmith in his book *Practicing the Presence* writes " [22] The spiritual life reveals clearly that God's grace is our sufficiency in all things. We do not need anything in this world except His grace" (p. 83). When we experience lack we are to declare unreservedly that "Thy Grace is my sufficiency." Jesus teaches us "Seek ye first the kingdom of God and all else will be given unto you."

In *Love Without End: Jesus Speaks* by Glenda Green [10] we read that Jesus told her that "at the center of your soul is the Sacred Heart. This is the point at which you are one with God. The heart sees infinity within and without…It can ascertain the origin of conditions and change them. The heart is your higher intelligence… Your mind is merely a servant and it behaves well if it is given positive impulses; it behaves very poorly if it is given negative impulses…It is from this power, within the center of your being that the entire script of your life is written. Live in your heart to either fulfill the script of your life or to rewrite it…The answers to healing your life will be found in the inner strength of your heart…Strengthen all of your positive emotions through daily gratitude and admirations. Disempower your negative emotions daily through forgiveness." (pp. 50-51).

Ernest Holmes in *Can We Talk To God?* [23] writes "The secret of spiritual power is a consciousness of one's union with the whole and the availability of good" (p. 58). I think that in Spiritual Mind Treatment the power comes from dropping into our Sacred Heart and realizing our Divinity and the Divinity of those we treat. We then affirm the reality of the Goodness that comes from that Divine Inheritance. We place the mind in its proper place as a servant to our positive thoughts thereby stimulating the Law of Life to create that which we know to be true.

My Prayer Partner

I have a wonderful Prayer Partner, Shayla. We became Prayer Partners when, at the end of my first Introductory Class at the Center for Spiritual Living, it was suggested we choose one. We turned to each other and made that commitment to each other.

It has been wonderful! I feel so blessed. We text or call each other every week on Sunday, after the Service, to ask for prayer. It is a simple request, but one that makes a huge difference in one' life. We offer each other support each week in remembering who we really. We have helped each other through a lot of rough spots. I would suggest everyone get one!

Show Me The Way

Show me the way. Show **me** the way.
Your love will light the way.
Show me the way. Show me the way.
Your love will light the way.
Nam..Nam..Nam..Namaste
Nam..Nam..Nam..Namaste
Namo..Namo..Namo..Namaste.

Show me the way. Show me the way.
Your love will light the way.
Show me the way. Show me the way.
Your love will light the way.
Nam..Nam..Nam..Namaste
Nam..Nam..Nam..Namaste
Namo..Namo..Namo..Namaste

Song by Karl Anthony.

The Ending

I have now been sober now for three years and five months. The process of Recovery and Spiritual Growth is a continuous one and I am sure I will continue to grow and change. However, I think the purpose of this book has been completed.

I hope that I have said something that will be beneficial to you. That has been my sincere purpose in writing it. I bless you on your spiritual journey.

Namaste,

Rose

Appendix A The Twelve Steps of Recovery

1. We admitted we were powerless over alcohol - that our lives had become unmanageable.
2. Came to believe that a power greater than ourselves could restore us to sanity
3. Made a decision to turn our will and our lives over to the care of God <u>as we understood Him.</u>
4. Made a searching and fearless more inventory of ourselves.
5. Admitted to God, to ourselves, and to another human being the exact nature of our wrongs.
6. Were entirely ready to have God removes all of these defects of character.
7. Humbly asked Him to removes our shortcomings
8. Made a list of all persons we had harmed, and became willing to make amends to them all.
9. Made direct amends to such people wherever possible except when to do so would injure them or others.
10. Continued to take personal inventory and when we were wrong, promptly admitted it.

11. Sought through prayer and meditation to improve our conscious contact with God <u>as we understood Him,</u> praying only for knowledge of His will for us and the power to carry that out.
12. Having had a spiritual awakening as the result of these steps, we tried to carry this message to alcoholics and to practice these principles in all of our affairs.

Appendix B
References

1. Caroline Myss, *Why People Don't Heal and How They Can.* (Pristine Publishing), 1998.
2. William James, *The Varieties of Religions Experience,* (Panthianos Classics), 1902, 1983.
3. Eknath Eshwaran, *The Upanishads,* (Nilgiri Press), 1987, 2007.
4. St. John of the Cross, Translation by Mirabai Starr, *Dark Night of the Soul.* (New York, Riverhead Books), 2002.
5. Caroline Myss, Entering the Castle: Finding the Inner Path to God and Your Soul's Purpose, (New York, Atria Paperback), 2013.
6. Stephen A. Hoeller, Forward by June Singer, *Jung and the Lost Gospels: Insights Into The Dead Sea Scrolls and the Nag Hammadi Library.* (Wheaton, Illinois, Chennai (Madras), India, Quest Books Theosophical Publishing House), 1989.
7. Marvin Meyer, Editor, The Nag Hammadi Scriptures: The Revised and Updated Translation of Sacred Gnostic Texts, (HarperCollins Publishers), 2007.
8. Apostolos N. Athanassakis and Benjamin M. Wolkow, *The Orphic Hymns: Translation, Introduction, ad Notes,* (Baltimore, Johns Hopkins
9. University Press), 2013.
10. Anonymous, *Alcoholics Anonymous,* (New York, New York, Alcoholics Anonymous World Services, Inc.), 1939, 1955, 1976,

. 2001.
11. Glenda Green, *Love Without End: Jesus Speaks,* (Fort Worth, TX, Heartwing Publishing), 1999.
12. Gary R. Renard, *The Disappearance of the Universe: Straight Talk about Illusions, Past Lives, Religion, Sex, Politics, and the Miracle of Forgiveness.* (Pristine Publishing), 2004.
13. Anonymous, *A Course in Miracles: A Combined Volume,* (Tiburon, California, Foundation for Inner Peace), 1975, 1985).
14. Wikipedia, Bill W.
15. Wikipedia, Dr. Bob
16. Ian McCabe, *Carl Jung and Alcoholics Anonymous.* (Pristine Publishing), 2015.
17. Frances Fuchs, *Private Email Correspondence,* (Santa Rosa, California), November, 2020
18. Ernest Holmes, *The Science of Mind: The Complete Edition,* (Jeremy R. Tharcher, Penguin), 1926, 1960.
19. Ralph Waldo Emerson, *Emerson's Essays: Introduction by Irwin Edman,* (Crown Company), 1926, 1951.
20. Thomas Troward, *The Edinburgh and Dore Lectures on Mental Sciences,* (Camarilla, CA, DeVorss Publications), 1904, 1909, 1989.
21. Emma Curtis Hopkins, *Scientific Christian: Mental Practice,* (Camarilla, CA, DeVorss Publications).
22. Emmet Fox, *Sermon on the Mount: The Key to Success in Life,* (Harper One), 1989.
23. Joel Goldsmith, *Practicing the Presence,* (Hawkins Books), 1987.
24. Ernest Holmes, *Can We Talk God,* (Deerfield Beach, FL, Health Communications Inc.), 1999.

Louse Hays, *How to Heal Your Body,* (Hays House Publishing), 1970.

Printed by Libri Plureos GmbH in Hamburg, Germany